Praise for *The Ikigai Way*

Do you find yourself wondering "is that all there is" after hitting your big life goals? Are happiness and purpose still eluding you? Or, are you stuck in the grind of the "shoulds" on your list wondering if you'll ever get to live life instead of life living you? David Marlow's *The Ikigai Way* is what you've been looking for: a step-by-step guide to the life you've always wanted answering the questions you never quite knew how to ask.

—April Shprintz
Business Accelerator, Creator of The Generosity Culture®
and Award-Winning Author of
Magic Blue Rocks: The Secret to Doing Anything
https://www.linkedin.com/in/aprilshprintz

For a couple of years now, David's personal, poignant musings on Ikigai have graced my weekly reading and given me a touchstone for professional reflection.

At a time when, as committed professionals, our personal and professional lives are inextricably interwoven . . . a battle, really, for the self . . . David's musings have been an inspiration to developing a centered, focused mindset, to align common priorities, and to craft a unified way forward as a whole person. I'm deeply grateful for his own deeply personal insights.

Now . . . a book! Nothing short of a roadmap . . . complete and orchestrated . . . to help guide us toward full potential for a balanced life. This book, like his weekly musings, will certainly become a touchstone for balance.

—Gordon RAY
Lecturer in Management, Technology, and Strategy,
Grenoble Ecole de Management
https://www.linkedin.com/in/gordon-ray

At last: The Ikigai Guy between two covers! For those people, like myself, who've been part of David Marlow's LinkedIn community these past few years, this publication is a welcome evolution. In these pages, you'll find generous helpings of Marlovian material: Etymologies galore! War stories from corporate life! Cute anecdotes about single-letter grandkids! A plethora of life lessons from running and the Marines! And then some! You ought to look into this *Way of Ikigai* thing.

—Ken Gordon
Chief Communications Specialist, EPAM Continuum
https://www.linkedin.com/in/gordonken

David Marlow is a gifted writer, highly accomplished leader, and a master of Ikigai who expertly guides people to connect with and joyfully live in alignment with their unique purpose. I find David's insights and sage storytelling to be immensely thought provoking and inspiring. I'm excited to delve deeper into the ideas he shares in his new book!

—**Andrea Choate**
Founder, Soul Mechanics Healing
https://www.linkedin.com/in/andreachoate

I've been a fan of David Marlow, as a person, social media influencer, and ardent follower of his work for nearly eight years. It's no exaggeration to say that he's one of the foremost authorities on the Japanese concept of IKIGAI.

Beyond his ability to personally connect with his audience, his writing is a masterful blend of precision and wit, never wasting a word yet always leaving you with a smile. I'm excited about reading his new book because I'm guaranteed that it will be another brilliant example of how he can capture my imagination while delivering profound insights.

I can't wait to get my hands on a copy, and you shouldn't hesitate to buy one either. Marlow's stuff is "must-read" for anyone seeking a deeper understanding of purpose and fulfillment.

—**Monte Pedersen**
Principal/Owner, The CDA Group LLC
https://www.linkedin.com/in/monte-pedersen-9554a1126

Dave entertains, instigates, educates and inspires. Sometimes he magically manages to do all of those things in a single paragraph or story. I'm thankful for his thoughtful, accessible approach to helping me uncover my purpose and embrace my Ikigai.

—**Mark Cumicek**
"The Dream Dude"
https://www.linkedin.com/in/markcumicek

In a world where we feel overrun and overwhelmed by options, or conflicted between aspirations and obstacles, comes the guidance of David Marlow and his Ikigai quest. From the moment you are able to grasp the concept as he lays it out, one feels that they have embarked on a trail where they can only see the rest of the path, and the next scene emerge around the corner, as we walk the first steps available to us. Uncovering one's reason for existence gradually impacts everything we do . . . on purpose.

—**Scott Boddie**
(Director of Organizational Development PATTERN4building)
Nationally Recognized Mental Health Advocate LinkedIn Top Voice
https://www.linkedin.com/in/scott-boddie

Unlock the power of your Ikigai with David Marlow's insightful and action-oriented debut. This book offers a profound vision of living one's Ikigai, paired with practical, manageable steps to make it a daily reality. It's an empowering read, designed to support and inspire readers in a refreshingly informal and approachable way, boosted with maximum clarity and momentum-building ideas.

—**Adam Hansen**
(author of *Outsmart Your Instincts: How the Behavioral Innovation Approach Drives Your Company Forward*)
https://www.linkedin.com/in/adhansen

Working with David Marlow to craft my Ikiverse has given me a powerful, life-changing tool that helps me live my purpose each day. My Ikiverse is a reminder of why I'm here, what's important to me, and how I can best spend my time and energy. Having my Ikiverse makes it easy for me to communicate my purpose and values to others, and it also serves as a touchstone for helping make sure my decisions are aligned with my Ikigai.

When I'm feeling lost or not quite myself, a read through my Ikiverse always brings me back to myself. It's become one of my favorite tools for knowing and staying true to myself. I will always be grateful for the gentle and supportive way David has helped me craft and live by my Ikiverse, and I'm excited to see the impact his new book will have on the world.

—**Amanda Stern**
(founder Good Things Come to Those Who Journal)
https://www.linkedin.com/in/amandasternjournaling

David Marlow possesses a singular talent for simplifying complex ideas in the form of practical, inspirational wisdom. His insights and observations are penetrating, ceaselessly relevant, and guaranteed to set you on course for living a more successful and satisfying life. You can't help but come away from his work with feelings of gratitude and exhilaration.

—**Rabbi Yonason Goldson**
(author of *Grappling With the Gray: An Ethical Handbook for Personal Success and Business Prosperity*)
https://www.linkedin.com/in/yonason-goldson

I've been reading Dave's writing for the past three years. Now you may think you know what this book is about when you see Ikigai on the cover. But I guarantee you'll be surprised by the originality and depth of Dave's thinking. As a bonus, his work is informed by decades of lived experience and peppered with humor. Read this book!

—**Kat (Katrijn) van Oudheusden**
(author of *Selfless Leadership: A Complete Guide to Awakening the Servant Leader Within*)
https://www.linkedin.com/in/katrijnvo

David is one of the most insightful, intuitive and brilliant thinkers I know in the area of purpose, Ikigai and strategy. He opened my eyes and gave me new perspectives around Ikigai that I hadn't considered. His writing, storytelling and teachings engage and inspire in a way that honors the learner and expands their thinking. You will want to keep this book with you as a resource and a guide throughout your life.

—**Jean Marie DiGiovanna**
(author of *Stop Talking Start Asking: 27 Questions to Shift the Culture of Your Organization*)
https://www.linkedin.com/in/jeanmariedigiovanna

In his book, David guides us on a journey to uncover a deeper self-understanding. He helps us rise above the noise and programming, rediscovering our essential selves to live from a place of inner wisdom and vitality.

This journey isn't prescriptive; rather, it offers a map and compass to reflect on our past and envision the future we wish to explore. The book's ideas are clear, concise catalysts for self-reflection, prompting us to question and disrupt self-limiting beliefs and outdated mental models that hold us back from answering life's bigger questions.

—**David McLean**
(Executive Counselor McLean & Company)
LinkedIn Top Voice 2022
https://www.linkedin.com/in/davidmcleanatgetkeepgrow

Dave's insights have always inspired me to push deeper, both personally and professionally. His unique approach to Ikigai is powerful yet accessible, making complex ideas feel approachable and transformative. I'm excited to explore these concepts further in his new book.

—**Rishita Jones MCIPD**
(Featured contributor BIZCATLYST 360° and LinkedIn Top Voice)

Ever since David Marlow and I were high school friends during his radio DJ days, I have appreciated David's humor, perspective, and outlook on life. He is a lifelong learner with a love of improving things and helping people discover their identity, gifts, and purpose. He is a great communicator with a knack for saying things in new ways that make sense. I know you'll appreciate this book!

—**Rev. Dr. Clark Cowden**
Senior Pastor, First Presbyterian Church of Hollywood, CA
https://www.linkedin.com/in/clark-cowden-042b19a;
https://clarkdcowden.wordpress.com

Having had a chance to preview David's book, I'm so excited for others to experience his process, tips, reflective questions, and abundant stories. As a follower of his work for several years, I learned so much more. It inspired me to spend time creating my Ikiverse!

—**Melissa Carson**
CEO Canopy Strategies, author of
A Perfect Life Is Not the Goal: A Practical Guide to Loving the Life You Are Living
and *There Is No Such Thing as a Perfect Job: A Practical Guide
to Loving Your Work Life*

Uncovering our Ikigai can be a confusing and, at times, disheartening experience, but David's guidance will make your own Ikigai journey just a little bit clearer. David thoughtfully unpacks what Ikigai means through a plethora of relatable stories and actionable frameworks. We all deserve a life that is filled with purpose—let David's book show you the way!

—**Peter Nakamura**
Host of The Ikigai Project podcast
https://www.linkedin.com/in/peternakamura;
https://shows.acast.com/6244f09bbac91e00126bad9a

David reminds me to treasure life. Although, I don't often heed his advice. The truth is that living purposefully is hardly a fairy tale. As a dad and a business owner, I'm probably doing it wrong more often than not.

And yet we persist. That's the point (I think). The point of living purposefully. Part of what I'm learning from him. To embrace life's challenges and appreciate the gift that is a life experienced daily.

He calls this Ikigai.

—**Daniel Furfaro**
(Founder and Brand Strategist at Brandmoves)

Dave showed me that every moment plays a part in my journey. Sometimes, you have to laugh, and sometimes, you have to frown, but it all makes sense in the big picture. That is why I love his Ikigai storytelling; his book triggers questions and motivates me to find answers.

—**Ivona Hirschi**
(LinkedIn Top Voice) Founder & Chief Content Officer leadink
https://www.linkedin.com/in/ivona-hirschi-05301270

The

Ikigai

Way

DAVID E. MARLOW

The

Ikigai

Way

A Simple Path for Living
a Life of Purpose

WILEY

Published by John Wiley & Sons, Inc., Hoboken, New Jersey.
Published simultaneously in Canada.

For general information on our other products and services or for technical support, please contact our Customer Care Department within the United States at (800) 762-2974, outside the United States at (317) 572-3993 or fax (317) 572-4002.

Wiley also publishes its books in a variety of electronic formats. Some content that appears in print may not be available in electronic formats. For more information about Wiley products, visit our web site at www.wiley.com.

Library of Congress Cataloging-in-Publication Data

Names: Marlow, David E., author.
Title: The Ikigai way : a simple path for living a life of purpose / David
    E. Marlow.
Description: Hoboken, New Jersey : John Wiley & Sons, Inc., [2025] |
    Includes bibliographical references and index.
Identifiers: LCCN 2024046641 (print) | LCCN 2024046642 (ebook) | ISBN
    9781394286522 (hardback) | ISBN 9781394289172 (adobe pdf) | ISBN
    9781394289165 (epub)
Subjects: LCSH: Self-realization. | Satisfaction. | Career development. |
    Conduct of life.
Classification: LCC BF637.S4 M2286 2025 (print) | LCC BF637.S4 (ebook) |
    DDC 158.1—dc23/eng/20241122
LC record available at https://lccn.loc.gov/2024046641
LC ebook record available at https://lccn.loc.gov/2024046642

Cover Design: Wiley
Cover Images: © Yasna /Adobe Stock Photos, © Hulinska Yevheniia / Adobe Stock Photos, © tina bits/Adobe Stock Photos
SKY10096998_012325

To everyone who has ever felt like they were created for something more.

Contents

Prologue

Begin, to Become

A SPIRIT ENTERS the creation as a child. A new beginning, innocent, not knowing the ways of this world. Immediately, the child needs lessons taught, and burdens placed so that it can operate in society. And as the young child learns the ways of this realm, it becomes a camel to bear the ever-heavier lessons and burdens.

Now, as a camel, it grows strong and mature, able to endure the weights it must carry. Each burden's increase is accompanied by a nod of approval from the world. The camel's pride soars with each plaudit even as the memory of life as a child begins to fade.

A quiet desperation falls on the camel as carrying the increasing lading, once thought of as a prodigious achievement, becomes too much. No longer willing to add obligations and unable to drop the burden it already carried, the camel seeks freedom by fleeing into the wilderness.

In the deepest, densest, darkest part of the primordial demesne, exhausted from running, the camel collapses. That is when the second transformation occurs. Lying on the mossy ground, the camel, its burden now vanished, becomes a lion.

Though no longer carrying the load of the camel, the lion is not yet free and must face an even bigger challenge. Reigning over the wilderness is a sparkling golden dragon; the great "Thou Shalt." Peerless in size, on every one of its scales of gold was each etched a "Thou Shalt." A thousand years of rules, and another thousand years of order glittered on those scales. And each "Thou Shalt" was written in the language of the default.

The lion followed the decrees of "Thou Shalt," fearful of the fire-breathing beast. Though strict and uncompromising the dragon provided security and a framework. For a time, the lion prospered in the wilderness.

Until one day the illusion and arbitrariness of this default space became too much to bear, and the lion declares it will be free, "I will," said the lion.

"Thou Shalt," bellowed the gilded behemoth, and a great battle began. The lion attacked the dragon, dodging blasts of fire to one by one remove the golden plates with his carnassial teeth. With each scale removed, the dragon weakened.

Though singed during every bout, the lion continued the fight until at last the final auric decree was removed and "Thou Shalt," the once fearsome lord of the wilderness fell to the forest floor never to move again.

With the dragon defeated, the lion returned to being a child. In the child was found once again, innocence, a life at play and still more. In the re-born child is a new beginning as a self-rolling wheel, a first movement, a holy yea to life as it was meant to be.

1

What Is Ikigai?

FROM CHILD TO camel to lion to child again with slaying a doyen dragon thrown in for good measure. The allegory presented in the prologue represents the three stages of inner transformation required to live a life of purpose: the taking back of our story.[1]

Ever feel like a thousand years of "Thou Shalt" scales have held you back? The demands of "shoulds," "have tos," and "oughts" keeping you from the life you want, from life as it was meant to be?

Those societal forces that are both necessary and restrictive are constraints we needed to survive that must be thrown off if we are to thrive. The process of removing the "Thou Shalts" is the Ikigai way. Before we commence slaying dragons, it is best to explain what Ikigai is and what it is not.

Ikigai is a Japanese compound word made up of two words, "iki," meaning life and "kai," loosely translated as reason, or reason to live. Through a unique characteristic of Japanese pronunciation when the two words are combined the "k" of "kai" transposes to "g" and becomes Ikigai.

It is pronounced with "E" as in a long ē, "key" as in what you use to unlock a door, and "guy," like the guy writing this book.

Ē•key•guy

If you search the internet, you are likely to come upon a four-circle Venn diagram in various incarnations espousing Ikigai as the intersection of four things.

3

- What you love (or are passionate about).
- What the world needs.
- What you are good at.
- What you can be paid to do.

There is some dispute as to the origin of both the diagram and the idea that your Ikigai can be found at the intersection of these four things.

Regardless of the origin, the "Venn Garden," as I like to call it, is not Ikigai in any traditional sense and has the additional problem of being focused exclusively on career.

While our careers and making a living are important, life is far more than our jobs. Professions come and go; our "reason for living" remains.

It would be accurate to say that Ikigai is a philosophically profound concept that's difficult to describe or define succinctly. While true, that isn't particularly helpful in understanding and embracing your life purpose. This book will support you by bridging the gap between the theoretical concept of Ikigai and its practical application.

Later in this chapter, I'll offer a richer, more comprehensive definition that will reconcile the abstract concept of the Venn Garden and the true meaning of Ikigai. We'll explore this in detail, but for now, let me illustrate the contrast through a story.

An Unexpected Miracle

My wife and I were blessed with two sons early in our marriage. After several years, we were informed by doctors that she couldn't have any more children, which we now know was due to complications related to multiple sclerosis. Lo and behold, six years after our youngest son was born my wife became pregnant again. Like the old Yiddish proverb, "Man plans, God laughs." Our miracle baby was a little girl and from the time she was born, our only daughter was determined to keep up with her two older brothers.

With her brothers playing baseball she started in T-ball. For those unfamiliar, T-ball is a beginner form of baseball. It introduces you to some basic concepts of the game but isn't the complete game. Both boys played on championship teams as kids with our youngest son ultimately playing in college. As a result, my daughter was used to watching people play the game at an advanced level.

Her T-ball career started off less than auspiciously as she is left-handed and the coach lined her up on the plate like a right-handed batter, the wrong side for her. As soon as he backed away, she switched sides and promptly hit the ball into center field well beyond any of the opposing players.

She ran to first base and kept going until somewhere on her way around all the bases a coach stopped her and sent her back to first. While we couldn't hear the conversation, still fuming, she would later recount, "I don't know why he stopped me, I totally could have scored." In T-ball they don't keep score, you can only go one base at a time, and there aren't positions. The ball is placed on a tee and players are allowed as many swings as they need to get a hit.

All of this frustrated my daughter, with the final indignity coming at the end of the season when she was given a "participation trophy" for being on the team. She wanted to play real games and tournaments and get a trophy for winning a championship, like her brothers.

Baseball, on the other hand, is a far more nuanced and rewarding experience. It allows you to uncover and develop many skills and get to know more about yourself and what you are made of as a person. There is strategy and drama, success and failure.

The Venn Garden is the T-ball version of Ikigai. Enough elements of the game to seem like the real thing though ultimately only a cursory experience. The equivalent of a participation trophy. Growth in Ikigai can be much like in other practices, such as learning a sport. You start small, and then, when ready, you take it to another level. If you are reading this, you are ready for the grown-up version of the game of Ikigai.

There are three fundamental questions we all seek to answer in life.

Who am I?

Why am I here?

What should I do?

This book supports you in answering those questions.

"There is a place in the soul that neither time nor space nor no created thing can touch."

—Meister Eckhart[2]

There is within us, something that transcends the superficial categorizations of skills and careers. It's this essence that forms the core of our Ikigai. As promised, I offer a richer, more comprehensive definition:

> *Ikigai is expressing your essence and purpose in harmony with whatever you do.*

Understanding Ikigai in this way breaks free of the constraints of defining ourselves solely by our careers or jobs. Framing Ikigai in this way supports our fundamental drive to answer those three most important questions: Who am I? Why am I here? What should I do?

Who Am I?

Ikigai begins with understanding your essence. The Latin root for essence is *esse* or "to be." Your essence is the most sacred core of who you are. That part of your nature without which you would not exist or be.

It is a place within, untouched by setbacks, sorrows, judgment, and pain. A place in the soul free of scars that is peaceful, confident, brave, and true. That exquisite untouched spirit is who you are and were always meant to be.

Why Am I Here?

Your purpose, the reason you are here, can be described as your intention, skills, gifts, talents, passions, and calling. There is a reason you were born, that is your purpose.

What Should I Do?

That is perhaps the most difficult of the three questions to answer. First you must understand that what you do isn't as important as how you do it. Whatever you do, whether working, walking, whipping up an egg breakfast, everything should be in service and harmony to who you are and why you are here.

Ikigai then isn't your purpose or your identity, it is a way and approach to live out your purpose and identity expressing them in every part of your life. Your Ikigai can be expressed in myriad ways and every aspect of life. In fact, expressing your essence and purpose in everything you do is Ikigai.

Those three questions we all want resolved of **Who, What,** *and* **Why** are answered *with* **Ikigai.**

- Who you are at your deepest levels. (Essence)
- Why you are here, your intention, gifts, talents, passions, and calling. (Purpose)
- What you are doing, in harmony with your essence and purpose. (Harmony)

The Ikigai Nexus

To further illustrate how Ikigai addresses these questions, I've developed the Ikigai Nexus (see Figure 1.1). This visual representation brings to life our definition of Ikigai: expressing your essence and purpose in harmony with whatever you do.

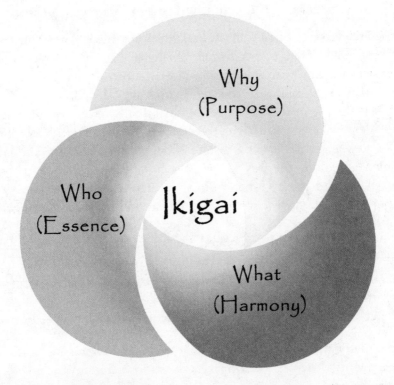

Figure 1.1   The Ikigai Nexus.

The original Latin meaning of nexus—"that which ties or binds together"—perfectly describes the connection and interdependence of Ikigai's elements. This framework maps out those interconnected elements, each influencing and reinforcing the others. When we express our essence and purpose harmoniously in everything we do we are experiencing our Ikigai—in our careers, our relationships, and our daily lives.

The Language of Default

There is a default language in life. The language of default is filled with *shoulds* and *have tos* and *ought tos* and *musts*.

default (n. & v.)

1. *(v.) To deceive, to cheat; to put wrong, to lead astray, cause to be mistaken; be concealed from.*
2. *(n.) A state of privation or deprivation in which things that are essential for human well-being are scarce or lacking.*[3]

When have you felt like your life and gifts were wasting away, misused, or consumed? That is the default, a language of disintegration and burnout. We are as the definition clearly shows, deceived, cheated, and led astray by following the well-worn way of default.

It is the use of this language that eventually covers up our Ikigai. The life we were meant to live, the one we were created for is obscured from view and what is left is a state of deprivation, scarcity, and lack. Somewhere along the way . . . we just began shutting down parts of ourselves to be able to function in this default space. The journey to Ikigai begins when we leave the default way and embrace the language and life of purpose.

When have you felt integrated, sound, whole, and complete? That is the language of purpose. The language of purpose breathes life back into us. It helps us uncover those hidden parts of ourselves long ago forgotten.

Let's look at the opposite, the antonyms of default:

- abundance
- plenty
- enough

- respect
- strength
- sufficiency
- satisfaction
- fulfillment

When we live from a point of purpose the whole world of possibilities open up for us. The life we were meant to live is revealed. There has never been a more disruptive time for careers. Between the changes brought on by the pandemic to the rupture of traditional models for careers, roughly three-quarters of people report experiencing burnout at work in the past year alone.

The majority of people over 50 (56%) will have their careers ended prematurely and nearly 90% of those will never make that level of salary again.[4] Younger people especially want meaning and purpose in their work. They also expect the companies they work for to have a defined purpose greater than making money. Yet every day we read about companies that have prioritized profits after promising employees and customers the sun, moon, and the stars.

Even companies with more than a century of commitment to their people are breaking their social contracts and kicking them to the curb with layoffs. Jobs come and go; who we become along the way is what lasts.

Two Halves of Life

Carl Jung popularized the idea of two halves to life. His thought being that the first half was about building the ego self—our careers, our identity, status, that sort of thing. This is what I call the default life, and it is driven by the language and expectations of the default. The *shoulds* and *have tos* and *ought tos* we are given from a young age.

Jung's perspective for a second half entailed either enlightenment or depression. Continuing the default path ultimately leads to disappointment and burnout. The second half of life can and should be focused and driven by the language of purpose rather than continuing the default.

How often were we advised to study hard and get good grades to obtain a good job? Keep moving up the ladder, build a career, and perhaps create a family. Then what? Most often, keep going forever or at least until retirement. For many, that is the default track the world has given us to take.

There is nothing wrong with good grades, building a career, or growing a family. When we ponder what is next and there is no next, we stay with the default. If we stay in the default or try to bridge the two, that is when we stagnate.

We become dissatisfied and burned out. Somewhere along the way we just began shutting down parts of ourselves to be able to function in this default space.

As I approached the second half of my own life, I felt an invitation to leave the default path. I had a highly successful career at the time, and it would have been easy for me to justify staying in that role. I didn't realize that in my efforts to balance my family and career priorities, I was inadvertently ignoring my own essence and purpose.

The essence of our lives is made real by the language we use. The second half of my life was calling, and I was drowning out the voice of purpose by reciting default language. There were times in my life when I balanced a high-stress job, the illness of a child, and being emotionally present for a disabled wife, all while trying to maintain everything else.

I coached my kid's sports, volunteered at church, and had a well-kept lawn . . . you get the idea. I became exceptional at compartmentalizing my feelings to juggle all those things.

When my son needed life-saving brain surgery, I buried the worry and kept going with everything else. People marveled that I was so calm under such circumstances. Neither they nor I realized at the time that I was living without integrity. Integrity, in this sense, meaning wholeness.

We live integrated lives when we are operating as the whole person in our Ikigai. When we try to "balance" rather than live in harmony with our essence and purpose, eventually, we start to disintegrate. Funny how in trying to "hold ourselves together" in such circumstances, we are contributing to our disintegration.

The default life is career centric and at some point begins to lack integrity. That is one reason why connecting Ikigai to career goes wrong for so many people. It is no small irony that focusing on career at the start may actually block you from finding one aligned with your

Ikigai. Whereas starting from a point of purpose will more likely lead to uncovering and living your Ikigai.

I used the word uncovering just now and this is a good time to explain why I choose that exact word. People want to find their purpose, find their calling, find their Ikigai. There is no need to find any of those things as they are already there, residing inside you.

Look at a child at play. Does it seem they need to find their true selves? Are they unable to know what their higher purpose is or how to be that self in everything they do? No, they live fully into who they are, why they are here in everything they do. You aren't lost where you need to be found. The real you, your true self, and essence are right here.

When we are young, our Ikigai is easy to see. Over time life happens with defeats, disappointments, and burdens piling on top of our true nature. Eventually, life conceals our Ikigai where it stays hidden, waiting.

Understanding your Ikigai is returning to that true self. It is a process of revelation and rediscovery. Seeing again what's always been there, fresh, and new. At least initially, the Ikigai Journey is an effort to remember who you were before the world told you who you should be.[5]

Our Ikigai gets buried by life. Loss, sorrow, criticism, disappointments, and even the words of well-meaning family and friends can create layers that cover and eventually hide our true selves. Looking for external validation creates another one of those layers and makes uncovering our Ikigai much more challenging. One way to break free is to take control of our story.

What This Book Is About

While much has been written about Ikigai this book is the first to explain how expressing your essence and purpose in harmony with whatever you do creates your Ikigai.

I come at these topics from the perspective of someone who has spent decades studying personal and business transformation. Through supporting thousands of people and dozens of organizations I've created a scaffolding structure that provides a foundation for learning Ikigai and then simple steps to start living it out in every aspect of your life.

This book will tell you how to incorporate meaning and purpose into your life, your work, and/or your business.

Most books either only touch on Ikigai at a high level and then combine it with some existing idea or stay so high level as to be exclusively generic and philosophical. The rare books that add in practical elements focus exclusively on careers. Ikigai is about every aspect of life.

This book will address the philosophical elements of Ikigai in meaningful ways as well as provide practical ways to incorporate it into every aspect of life.

Where We Will Begin

The book will be broken down into the Three Invitations of Ikigai.

1. Getting the Noise Down.
2. Uncovering your Purpose.
3. Living out your Ikigai.

The first invitation will teach you about the importance of getting the noise down so you can hear the still quiet voice of Ikigai. You'll learn a simple technique for reducing the noise in your life.

In the default world the noise drains us of focus, energy, and capacity, creating more distraction leading to mistakes, stress, and burnout. Once this cycle starts it becomes self-perpetuating vicious cycle of over-burden and noise.

Getting the noise level down allows for increased focus, energy, and capacity to invest in a deeper understanding of our life's meaning and purpose. This creates the flywheel of a virtuous cycle of ever deepening understanding, fulfillment, and opportunity to uncover our Ikigai, which is what we will do in the second invitation.

The third invitation builds on the lessons from the first two sections to show you how to live out your Ikigai, sharing your gifts with the world. This invitation will get that virtuous flywheel spinning, enabling you to express your Ikigai in every area of your life.

Things to Know

Throughout the book, there will be a mix of stories, examples, tools, and techniques. I've found that stories and real-life examples work best, especially with Ikigai. I share examples because, without models, the understanding of Ikigai is reduced to self-help platitudes. Many of these are from my own life. They will involve things like my love of coffee, running, and my grandchildren.

Let me say upfront, those are elements of my Ikigai. A coaching client after working with me jokingly wondered if they had to love running to uncover their Ikigai. You don't have to love any of the things I do, though you'd be hard-pressed not to love my grandkids . . . they are adorable!

When building hobbies, practices, and habits, choose harmony over content. I like running and coffee. By aligning things *you* enjoy with what *you* do, you'll find harmony and connect with your Ikigai.

The Ikigai I teach is not a religion but a philosophy that is compatible with and inclusive of all faith traditions. Throughout the book, I will draw upon the wisdom of many cultures, faiths, and practices, sharing ideas from various perspectives, including my own. The intention is to make Ikigai accessible, relatable, and inviting to everyone, regardless of their background or beliefs.

This book encapsulates the lessons I've learned in my 20+ year journey to Ikigai and is designed to support you in accelerating your own journey, uncovering and living your best life.

2

If You Were Done

"Dave, I'm lost. I don't know who I am."

MATT[1] HAD BEEN with the company since graduating from college. Successful in whatever he pursued, he moved steadily up the leadership ranks. Only a few years ago, it looked like he might even become number two behind only the CEO.

Now we were going down on the same elevator, literally and figuratively as our department was dissolved and our jobs with it. Technically, it was early retirement, though we both knew what it really meant.

This was an executive of one of the most storied companies in America, and he wasn't sure who he was because his job had been eliminated.

Having been given the same news, I wasn't shocked, upset, or lost. In fact, aside from feeling sympathy for Matt, I was experiencing a kind of peace that comes from knowing who you are and why you are here. A peace that transcended the satisfaction and identity of a job. The difference between us in that moment and how you can experience it is what this book is about.

My journey began with a dream. I'm sure you had one of these where you can't get it out of your head when you wake up. It has been over two decades, and I still remember it.

One of the interesting things about the dream was Steve Mariucci. You may know Steve Mariucci as an announcer on the NFL Network, though at the time he was the head coach of the San Francisco 49ers football team. I don't know him, so it's interesting that he was talking to me in a dream.

In the dream, Mariucci comes to me and asks, "David, what would you do if you were done?" I remember being taken aback by the question and responding, "What?" Mariucci asked again, "What would you do if you were done?"

Immediately after he asked the second time, I woke up. As you may have guessed, I spent a lot of time pondering the meaning of such a dream. Done with what, I wondered?

What's Next?

I was 40 years old and had hit my stride. I was happily married and blessed with three kids. My two sons were in high school at the time, and my youngest, our daughter, was starting elementary. In my career I was a vice president at a large Fortune 500 company. I led an IT department whose datacenter handled 20% of all the financial transactions in the United States each day.

We'd had so much success that I spoke at AT&T's National Customer Conference in New York, giving the keynote address. This was to all the CEOs and CIOs of AT&T's biggest customers, who at the time represented many of the biggest companies in the world. At the pinnacle of life, in my dream, I was being asked by a football coach of a team I didn't even follow, what would I do if I were done? Everything up to that point had been along the traditional path. Being done meant a next and there was no obvious next.

I started exploring and looking into all aspects of my life. In only 18 months on the job, I had taken a failed department that was at risk of being outsourced to one making up one-third of the total company revenue. Despite things going well there was stress. My job was filled with extreme pressure. I was on call 24 hours a day, seven days a week. For all that I received an underwhelming $20,000 bonus.

Even with all the job demands I managed to make home life a priority. For years I had coached all my kids in sports. When I had taken the job, I decided to endure a long commute rather than move closer to work to avoid disruption at home. On the drive I'd call my wife and that would be our "catch-up" time, because as soon as I hit the doorway the kids wanted my attention.

The dream prompted me to consider what aspects of my life I could or should be "done" with. What if I were done with my career? What might I want to do then? How would that impact what I could do in other areas of my life? I began experimenting. And I didn't know it at the time, but I was doing my purpose work. I was beginning to dive into why was I here, what was my purpose, and what were the deeper things?

It forced me to explore some other avenues in both my career and personal life. And one of those was to do consulting. I did start consulting, and through it I was offered a chance to get into a business with an equity stake in the company. As I mentioned, I had taken a department that was losing money to making millions in a matter of 18 months and had only received a small bonus.

In addition, my oldest son had brain surgery and was going to need our financial support for a significant portion of his life. My wife was showing signs of what we now know is MS. I felt I needed to be "done" with making money for other people and go all in to support my family in a bigger way.

I gave it all up by leaving a well-established career and going into a business partnership with someone who then promptly ripped me off.

Faced with no job and no business, I reset my career by starting all over at the company I ultimately ended my corporate career with, Northwestern Mutual (NM). I did some consulting work for them. That transitioned to becoming an employee as an individual contributor and eventually moving up into a management role.

By starting all over at NM, I found another opportunity to reflect on the question: "What if I was done?" I'd been with GE when it was the biggest company in the world and some other high-powered, high-intensity companies. NM was a much more laid-back culture and didn't require 70-hour weeks and that kind of thing. Because the NM culture was very different than the companies I'd worked for prior, there wasn't the same pressure as in my previous roles. It gave me a chance to reflect on whether I wanted that kind of career again.

They also didn't value outside experience. Being in senior leadership of some of the best-known companies in the world had little value to them, which would mean proving myself all over again. I decided to embrace that challenge for a while and use it as a time of reflection. The former Marine in me was just confident enough to think I could do it all again starting at the bottom and become a vice president of yet another storied company.

Career Epiphany

Which brings me to the second milestone on my Ikigai journey. Promotions had come in record time at NM and soon I was back in senior leadership. I developed a reputation for taking over underperforming teams and turning them around. Not only turning them around, doing it in a way that fit the culture and developed people on the team. While enjoying hitting the numbers and goals, helping the people grow and succeed in their personal and professional lives was even more fulfilling.

The company was transitioning from strictly life insurance to a full financial services company. Making that change meant having a network and web presence available 24 hours a day, 7 days a week. This would mean the IT team had to change. Though the transition had been underway for several years, little progress had been made in making the operational changes necessary to deliver the new levels of service required.

The existing management team had no experience delivering in an always-on environment. My experience in previous companies delivering high-availability IT services and my track record of successfully transforming teams and cultures made me the ideal candidate to lead the network support team through this transition.

Before I took over, engineers were making major changes to the network during the middle of the day. If something went wrong the whole network might go down. That was no longer acceptable. Changes needed to be planned and executed flawlessly. Many people doubted this team could make this transition and had warned me not to take the job.

It took some time, and admittedly I wasn't the most popular guy in the department for a while. Eventually the team came to see the value in a more disciplined approach and embraced it. We were becoming an effective team all around.

Our team's increasing effectiveness was put to the ultimate test when we were tasked with a complex and critical project: reconnecting every software application in the company to the network with new internet addresses.

There wasn't a list of every app even available. If the apps weren't identified and adjustments made by a certain date the existing addresses would be invalid and the app would fail.

The same team only a year earlier while repairing one of the two fiber optic cables between campuses accidentally cut the working cable, shutting down the entire company for a day, costing millions of dollars.

In the end, 438 software applications were identified, systems configured, networking changes made, and more. At 8:30 a.m. on the day of the deadline, every application in the company was up and running flawlessly.

Dead Inside

This was the kind of thing I lived for: coaching, mentoring, and leading a team of people to be the best that they could be. Enabling them to succeed in their life and their careers, to show that great things could be done by anyone.

And yet, at 8:31 a.m., standing in the middle of my team celebrating our biggest win to date—a project that had firmly reestablished my career—I wasn't excited or thrilled or any of the things I'd been in the past. I was sort of relieved. Something had changed in me. While I still enjoyed the coaching and mentoring, teaching, and helping our customers, I couldn't help but think that there was something more. Then my shoulder started hurting.

Tossing a Ball

It felt like a knife was being plunged into my shoulder as the doctor moved my arm. "Did you have an injury?" he asked, continuing to move my arm. There was no injury. One day my shoulder started hurting. It worsened over several months until it was almost unbearable. Since there was no injury, I asked, how does something like this happen?

He answered, "When you get to be your age . . ." *Ouch!* It suddenly hurt even worse. We tried months of physical therapy to no avail. Ultimately the decision was made to have rotator cuff surgery. It seemed straightforward what would be done, so I was taken aback when the doctor asked me about my goals.

He needed to know what I wanted to be able to do. "Goals?" I asked. The strategy for the surgery and my treatment plan would be dependent on what I wanted to be able to do with my shoulder. Some people in their late forties, like I was at the time, were satisfied with reaching up to a cabinet and getting a cup. Others liked to mountain climb.

"I want to play catch with my grandkids." It wasn't something I'd explicitly considered before. The words flowed effortlessly and without conscious intention out of my mouth, generated by a deep desire hidden until that moment, even from me. This was years before my kids were married, let alone parents to any grandchildren.

My department was coming up on a leadership reorganization, which meant I would be transitioning to a new role. Since I would be out for three months recovering from surgery, given the importance and demanding nature of the role, my boss decided I would turn over my duties to another manager ahead of time. This would allow plenty of time for me to get the new manager up to speed and connected with the team.

Because the plans for the organization structure weren't finalized, I didn't have another job assigned before the surgery. Having turned everything over, my time off allowed me to relax without a job or money to worry about. I was still being paid and knew I'd have a role when I returned. Since I didn't know what my future job would be I couldn't even involve myself in wondering what I should be doing or thinking about.

Being out on disability, I wasn't even allowed to log into my laptop, check email or anything work related. I was home, and my routine after the surgery was an hour of physical therapy, then an hour of icing.

I'd ice my shoulder and read, or I would write and then do another hour of PT or some other exercise. That's also when I restarted my running habit.

There was uninterrupted time with my wife, and I was available for my kids more. Without the stress of work, I was completely available emotionally. It was one of the most present times I can recall in my life. The first time since I was 16 years old that I didn't have some accountability that was work related.

This is the Life I Want!

I remember at one point thinking, I want this, to be able to work on the things I want to work on, take care of my body, get physically and spiritually fit, and maintain it. I wanted to be present for my wife and kids and friends. Nearing the end of my time off, I decided that this was the life I not only want, it was the life I would have.

It became a turning point in my life and career. I was assigned an interesting new job within the department. While doing that one, I convinced the executives at that company that we needed to make a dramatic culture change emphasizing quality, continuous improvement, and innovation. I proposed a Lean Transformation modeled on what Toyota has done. This represented something that had never been attempted before in a life insurance company. It would mean taking a company whose culture was resistant to change and completely redesigning operations. By eliminating waste, increasing quality, and instilling an ethos of continuous improvement across the organization we transformed a storied company that was set in its ways into one focused on improving and innovating.

This was my dream job. Creating and then growing a team whose entire purpose was to help others have better, more impactful lives and careers. All while providing more value for the customers, community, and the company. We were changing lives for the better every day.

Lean transformations can go on for decades for those of you who don't know. Toyota has been doing it for nearly three-quarters of a century. Most companies, though, get a little tired after about seven years.

It was becoming clear to me that ours was winding down. I could start to see that my career would probably not end the way I had hoped. My intention had been to keep doing this work, move into being a vice president then retire from the company five years later. Now I could see it wasn't going to work out that way. The company was changing. The culture was moving from being a place where you could have a lifelong career to more like a GE.

Layoffs began even though the economy was strong, and the company was prospering. I started writing on LinkedIn because I knew that the worst time to try and network is when you're actively looking for a job. I wanted to be proactive and build relationships while I was still employed.

Not needing a job gave me the opportunity to write, to share ideas and to connect with other people without any kind of agenda. Because the writing represented my raw thoughts and concepts, I asked some friends and colleagues for their impressions: "What do you think my brand is? How am I coming across?"

I received some feedback and insights. The specific feedback from one friend in particular, Ken Gordon,[2] had a profound impact on my life.

"I don't know about your brand, but you ought to look into this Ikigai thing," Ken said. I asked him what Ikigai was, and he added only that I should look into it. Of course I did investigate it. Suddenly a connection was made to all the work I had been doing since the dream.

It was a breathtaking epiphany when I officially learned about Ikigai, even though I had been on an Ikigai journey for over two decades without realizing it. The purpose work, the search for connection between my life and my purpose—all came together in the concept of Ikigai.

A New Beginning

As predicted, my corporate career did not end with a vice presidency. My division was eliminated and with it my job.

The new vice president met with me and offered me two options: another job, or I could take early retirement. Now, here is a critical point. For years I had done the work and formalized my understanding of my purpose.

I knew the kind of role that would enrich my life and what wouldn't. The opportunity they offered wasn't a bad job, but it would've been soul crushing for me because it just wasn't anything that I enjoyed doing or was called to do.

Because I understood my Ikigai, I was prepared to say no to that and take the risk of early retirement and starting my business. Compare that to my friend in the elevator. He was completely devastated because his entire self-image was built around that career.

In the elevator he said, "Dave, I don't know what to do. I don't even know who I am. This is the only company I've ever known. Now I don't know what I'm supposed to do."

That is key as we talk about purpose. Because I understood mine, I was equipped and prepared to deal with those changes. Jobs come and go. People come and go. Circumstances change, but your purpose remains. When you have that, you have the foundation to build a happy life. The great irony is that in Matt's moment of greatest confusion I was about to live the dream life I had imagined all those years ago when recovering from surgery.

Uncovering your Ikigai can take a long time when you're randomly doing it or waiting for life events to happen. A dream, business failure, shoulder surgery, a layoff, with some big gaps in between led me to my calling. The good news is it doesn't have to be that way for you.

In the following chapters, I'll share the insights, tools, and techniques I've gathered over my own journey to Ikigai. By exploring the wisdom of various cultures, faiths, and practices, and learning from real-life examples, you'll be equipped to accelerate your own journey of self-discovery. Together, we'll uncover the path to your best life—a life filled with purpose, passion, and fulfillment. Are you ready to embark on this transformative journey?

Let's get started.

3

The Three Invitations

"The things to do are: the things that need doing, that you see need to be done, and that no one else seems to see need to be done. Then you will conceive your own way of doing that which needs to be done—that no one else has told you to do or how to do it. This will bring out the real you that often gets buried inside a character that has acquired a superficial array of behaviors induced or imposed by others on the individual."
—Buckminster Fuller[1]

As CHILDREN, MANY of us have an innate sense of who we are and why we are here—operating harmoniously at that unique intersection in whatever we do. As we grow older, life's dragons have a way of piling things on top of that sense of self and purpose. As Buckminster Fuller noted, we take on a character, a role, and play a part of superficial behaviors designed to garner acceptance by those around us and the world in general.

The more hard-wired the default image and behaviors become the deeper that pristine sense of self gets buried. Before long, our true essence becomes something obscured and forgotten. We long for it though only the ghost of a distant memory remains. The longer it remains covered the harder it is to uncover later and the less likely it is we will return to that place of purity and purpose.

My quest to uncover my Ikigai took over 20 years and was characterized by aleatory twists and turns. Random ups and downs, misses and near misses, success, and failure along the way. While randomness is certainly true of life in general and can play a role in learning, it's neither the fastest nor most effective approach. In my many years of leading people and businesses through transformation, I've found there are three progressive levels of learning and understanding that provide wayfinding, accelerating our quest to Ikigai.

You've experienced that feeling, that sense of something more. It's a gentle voice calling you to remove the debris of life and live out who you are, why you are here in harmony with whatever you do. It whispers three invitations to the life you were meant to live.

These three invitations represent the progressive levels of transformation and change. I call them the Three Invitations of Ikigai.

1. Getting the Noise Down.
2. Uncovering your Purpose.
3. Living out your Ikigai.

An Invitation

As you might have guessed, these invitations are more than being asked to attend or participate in something. To fully understand the significance, we'll engage in distinction work—a powerful practice of examining words and concepts more deeply that you will use throughout your Ikigai journey.

By going beyond the surface definitions and common usage to the origins of words, we uncover layers of meaning hidden by the language of default. The word "invitation" provides us with our first opportunity.

Exploring the origins of "invitation" reveals root meanings that speak of summoning someone to a challenge, a feast, or to be entertained. Some of the oldest meanings suggest an invitation encourages someone to go after something, to pursue it with energy and enthusiasm.

The Three Invitations of Ikigai do that and more. They summon you to perhaps the greatest challenge you will face—uncovering and living out your Ikigai. Once uncovered, you are invited to feast on and be entertained by the life you were always meant to live. By accepting and acting upon these invitations, you'll gain the clarity and direction to pursue the life you were meant to live.

It is often posited that the two most important days in your life are the day you are born and the day you find out why.[2] Permit me to add a third day. The day you remove everything that distracts you from that purpose. That is when life becomes real and the quest for Ikigai can truly begin. Embracing and acting on these three invitations is how you have both those second and third days in your life. That is how we will slay the dragon of "Thou Shalt."

The remainder of this book explores the Three Invitations of Ikigai in depth. While everyone's quest is unique, the Three Invitations provide a systematic framework to guide you along the way. They represent foundational practices and approaches that support you on your unique path. They are presented in this order with intention, the acceptance of each preparing you for the next.

The first invitation focuses on quieting the noise, creating space for self-reflection and inner wisdom. You'll learn a simple though potent technique for reducing the noise in your life. In the default world the noise drains us of focus, energy, and capacity, creating more distraction leading to mistakes, stress, and burnout. Once this cycle starts it becomes a self-perpetuating vicious cycle of over-burden and stress.

Getting the noise level down allows for increased focus, energy, and capacity to invest in a deeper understanding of our life's meaning and purpose. This creates the flywheel of a virtuous cycle of ever deepening understanding, fulfillment, and opportunity to uncover our purpose, which is what we will do in Part II.

The Second Invitation guides you to clearly defining and articulating your purpose. This is by far the most challenging task for most people. People struggle for years, especially those using the Venn Garden, and often never uncover their hidden purpose. Through years of refinement, I've created an easy way to uncover and articulate your purpose.

This distinction is crucial because uncovering your purpose is just the first step. Being able to clearly articulate it is what allows you to truly embrace and live it. When you can express your purpose in a way that is authentic, compelling, and easily understood, you experience that "aha moment"—a profound sense of clarity and alignment that propels you forward on your Ikigai journey. We can begin to refine our understanding of what our purpose is.

The Third Invitation builds on the lessons of the first two invitations. This portion centers on living out your essence and purpose by sharing your gifts with the world. It is here we will get that virtuous flywheel spinning, enabling you to express your Ikigai in every area of your life.

Uzumaki and the Three Invitations

As we explore these Three Invitations, it's important to understand them through the lens of Uzumaki—a concept represented by a swirling spiral (see Figure 3.1). Uzumaki means "swirl" and speaks to creating and refining your understanding of Ikigai as you progress through each invitation.

Figure 3.1   The Uzumaki Swirl.

The symbol starts on the outside and moves ever inward. As the movement goes inward, your understanding is refined, tightened, and made deeper. Your passage through the Three Invitations of Ikigai is much like this. You'll start at a point on the edge with Getting the Noise Down. As you progress through Uncovering your Purpose and Living out your Ikigai, you'll be traveling the path of the spiral. Your understanding will be refined, and you'll narrow in on a progressively deeper grasp of your essence and purpose.

That is what the Uzumaki symbol represents in our broader Ikigai journey. You're starting at a great spot by engaging with these invitations. Because you are reading this book, you're beginning the Uzumaki process and frankly shortening the time it takes to get a deeper understanding through this reflection.

Uzumaki also serves as an invitation to always be learning, growing, and gaining greater clarity. The symbol serves as a visual reminder that this process is ongoing with each invitation serving as a turn of the spiral. Here's how the first invitation sets the stage.

Getting the Noise Down

Reducing the noise is foundational to creating the mental and emotional capacity necessary for the deeper work to come. Here's why getting the noise down is such an urgent first step.

Noise is everywhere in our lives, from notifications, social media, and news to visual clutter and the demands of operating in an ever-changing world. Other noise sources are those voices in our heads. Voices of fear, judgment, hurt, anger, disappointment, and more. Still more are the demands of our time energy from the language of default. Our jobs, even our own ambitions can generate distracting levels of noise.

As an engineer, I worked on sophisticated electronic gear transmitting and receiving radio signals. Having a clear signal was crucial for the systems to function properly. The signal would get drowned out if electronic interference, defective components, or other electronic noise sources were present. You've experienced this yourself if you've ever tried listening to an AM radio while driving under power lines. The static is so intense it overpowers the music.

Another way to think of it is to imagine yourself at a party or a crowded room with multiple conversations going on at high volume. The louder everyone talks the harder it is to hear, so people respond by talking even louder.

Our lives can get like that. The world has become so static-filled that it drowns out the necessary signal. Like the noise-filled room, everything in our lives has to be ever louder to get any attention. Sometimes, it's hard to think, let alone thrive and live into our Ikigai. Who has the mental space to ponder their life's true calling when they're constantly weighed down by the distraction of noise?

Burnout is nearing epidemic levels. A recent survey found that as many as 89% of people reported experiencing burnout in the past year.[3] Noise is a root cause of burnout and significantly impacts our relationships, work, and overall well-being.

We have to get the noise level down to hear that still, small voice of purpose. Reducing the noise in your life makes it much easier to be present for yourself and those you care about. You have the energy and focus on living your best life.

While there are many ways to reduce the noise, there's nothing like a defined process for beginning something. That's why I've carefully crafted the Seven Rituals of Calm for you. These rituals are designed to lay a foundation of calm in your life by reducing noise and keeping it down.

Accepting this invitation is your first step on the Uzumaki toward realizing the fullness of your Ikigai. Let's get started.

PART

I

The First Invitation
Getting the Noise Down

4

The Seven Rituals of Calm

"Grace means suddenly you're in a different universe from the one where you were stuck, and there was absolutely no way for you to get there on your own."

—Anne Lamott[1]

THE SEVEN RITUALS of Calm are specifically designed to get the noise down. By incorporating these simple practices you will cultivate an attitude of calmness, bringing more harmony into your day.

Great care was taken in creating these rituals to make them easy to do, ensuring that anyone can adopt them and start experiencing the benefits right away.

The Importance of Ritual

The word ritual crosses cultures and eras. In some of its earliest meanings it was an act of deliberation, consideration, and fitting together. A ritual is different than a habit in many ways. A habit is as the name implies, habitual. It is done without much thought or planning.

A ritual is intentional in nature, and while elements of ritual may be done routinely, it is the mindset, meaning, and aim that separate a ritual from something done as part of a routine.

A ritual can provide a point of demarcation, a memorable before or after. Approaching your practice as a ritual can also give it a deeper meaning and significance beyond just going through the motions. By getting the noise down in your life, these seven rituals will help you "fit together" your essence and purpose in harmony with whatever you do.

1. Kaizen
2. Shizuka
3. Ippuku
4. Mujo
5. Kanasha
6. Yasuragi
7. Isshin Furan

Ritual 1: Kaizen

Kaizen is a Japanese word that combines "kai" (change) and "zen" (good). It's often translated as "continuous improvement," though it can also mean "small change" or "small improvement."

Embrace the Gift of Small Beginnings   Think of anything in your life you've gotten better at doing or understanding. Without exception, you didn't start as an expert or anything even remotely like that. The idea of Kaizen is to continuously improve through small incremental changes; you embrace the learning that comes from starting small. Starting small, making errors, and learning along the way are the beginning of mastery.

In business and manufacturing, Kaizen is used to drive change and innovation. There is a place for that, and it works well. I've used it for decades to improve products and companies in my work.

For uncovering and living into our Ikigai the focus of Kaizen is eliminating fear and feelings of being overwhelmed or inadequate. When faced with a big thing like uncovering your life purpose, we can easily become overwhelmed. Instead, we want to focus on being a little better each day.

Why Small?   When faced with a significant change in our lives, fear kicks in. I started running again to help heal my shoulder. Imagine if I had been told I had to run a marathon or a thousand miles a year, I would have stopped before I even got started.

Yet through this process of Kaizen, I have accomplished both running a marathon and many times running over 1,000 miles in a calendar year. Here's how I went from being an out-of-shape man approaching 50 to running a marathon.

Running as Rehab   As part of the healing process after my rotator cuff surgery, doctors advised me to do something "brisk" to get blood flowing to the tendons in my right shoulder. With my arm still in a sling, I began walking briskly.

When I no longer needed the sling, I added in moving my arms quickly as I walked. My daughter was in high school at the time and an all-state cross-country runner. I thought if I started running again it would give us something to share.

I had run quite a bit when I served in the Marine Corps but that had been many years prior. It also wasn't the best way to learn to run since there was no training or technique, simply a lot of yelling to run faster.

Well versed in Kaizen, I started small and with no expectation as to results. I ran for one minute, walked for four, and repeated that once. That was it. Many people when trying to run will push too hard, get sore and then quit. My own tendency is to go all out at something, which has frequently led to overreaching.

In my coaching I often share something running great Jeff Galloway said about his own beginning in running, "Before I began running the idea that I'd ever go a mile seemed impossible. And of course, it was, until I ran a mile."[2]

I literally ran for one minute and walked for four and repeated it. That was my beginning. At that point, like Galloway, it was hard to imagine I could ever run a mile again.

Applying Kaizen, I gave myself permission to be terrible at the start and believe me I was. My form was bad, speed slow, and running for only a minute before walking I wasn't even doing much running. A mile seemed a mil . . . well, a long way away.

By making my first run something small, it made certain I was not sore or, worse, injured. This enabled a run the next day. One minute running, four minutes walking, repeat.

This was my routine for several days before I added another 30 seconds of running. Now it was one and a half minutes of running with three and a half minutes of walking and repeating.

Over time, the running ratio slowly increased, until I was at four minutes of running to one walking. Eventually, I added in a third sequence. Each time making only a change small enough to avoid inducing fear or creating soreness or injury that would cause me to stop running.

In no time, my daughter and I were running races together. To be clear, we *started* races together. She was out of view early in the race.

Once again, even in preparing for my first race I applied Kaizen. A small easily attainable goal of starting and finishing was my only objective. My time didn't matter, only that I finished. Even if I walked the last half, I gave myself permission to only need to finish.

Kaizen was how I trained for the race as well. Slowly increasing my mileage mixing running and walking until I was more than capable of completing a 5k or just over three miles.

I'm in my sixties now and have been running almost daily for over a decade without a single running injury. All because at each point along the way, I've focused on small changes. Small changes allowed me to begin. It began, and then it became.

Applying Kaizen to Routine Tasks   Let's explore another application of Kaizen. This time in doing something routine that seems overwhelming, like painting your house.

A while back I needed to paint my house and didn't want to do it, wanting to do a thousand other things instead. I saw it as a big job and felt overwhelmed. Here's how I did it.

I committed to doing small things and only those things, telling myself, "I'm going to remove the brass numbers and flag holder."

Done.

"Not so bad. I'm going to get all the materials together, and that is all."

Done.

"Still not bad. I will commit to getting this small portion done by the front door."

Done.

"That only took a few minutes, and the stuff is out; I'm going to do the other side of the door."

You see where this is going. I ended up doing the entire front of the house. I had been fighting this for weeks, always seeing it as a "big" job. Breaking it down into chunks made each one manageable, and I could see myself doing those small chunks.

I eliminated feelings of fear and being overwhelmed by only committing to doing one small next thing. Facing something overwhelming in your life? Break it down into small achievable chunks.

Kaizen helps us work through the limits we place on ourselves from the language of default.

Writing the Ikigai Way as an Example   When I started working on this book the voices in my head simultaneously told me it had to be perfect and that it couldn't be perfect. Because the idea of writing a book seemed overwhelming, I took a mental step back and asked myself what's one small thing I could do.

"I can do a terrible version."

When facing any feelings of resistance, especially with writing, I give myself permission to write something "terrible." I will sometimes actually type the words . . . *I'm writing a terrible paragraph and here it goes.*

Giving myself permission to have no expectation of greatness at the start freed me from staring at a screen all day, waiting for it to be perfect. On top of that, even those initial pages weren't terrible anyway.

I also broke down the beginning into three smaller chunks. That allowed me to do three smaller pieces of writing. As it turned out, that was the best way to format this book anyway!

Five things to know about Kaizen:

- Kaizen is a process of doing things using small steps.
- Small steps can lead to big changes.
- Using Kaizen lowers our fear response and quiets the noise.
- By embracing a terrible version, we give ourselves permission to be bad at the beginning when learning or doing new things.
- With small steps that seem insignificant, you'll gain habits and skills that will enable your more significant outcomes.

Sometimes the most minor step in the right direction ends up being the biggest step of your life.

Reflection

What are you facing or need to do right now?

What small questions need to be asked and answered in this situation?

What is the smallest thing you could do to take a step toward completing it?

Give yourself permission to do a terrible version to get started.

Above all else . . . start small . . . and start.

I began the Seven Rituals with Kaizen because it can feel overwhelming to think about incorporating all seven at once. Learning to start small keeps the fear of doing something new to a minimum. Also, using Kaizen will immediately help drop the noise level in your life and support all six of the other rituals.

Now that you've read Ritual 1: Kaizen, continue and read the remaining six rituals. Remember, everything starts small. There is no right or wrong way to explore these practices. One easy way to get started is to read each of the remaining rituals in order. Then return to the first ritual and focus on the learning and reflection for a day.

The next day go to the second ritual and do the same until you've gone seven days and touched on each ritual. One small step is all you need to get started. Once you get going, repeat the process for several weeks or pick one to focus on for an entire week.

As with Kaizen, gives yourself permission to start small and even "terrible." No pressure, just presence.

In the spirit of Kaizen, I' ll repeat these simple instructions after the seventh ritual to make getting started a small(er) thing.

Ritual 2: Shizuka

Shizuka means quiet in the sense of tranquility and peace. Look for places in your day to include quiet. I practice a Shizukana asa (Quiet Morning) routine.

I wake up easing into the morning, rarely waking up to an alarm. When I use an alarm, ample time is built in so I can perform my standard practice without rushing. I lay in bed, centering my thoughts—taking a moment to pray, express gratitude, and set my intention for the day.

Slowly getting up from bed, I avoid any sudden movements or rushing. Some days I stretch first; others, I start writing. The specific thing you do isn't as important as how you do it. The ritual is about bringing quiet, tranquility, and peace into whatever you do.

I turn on the espresso machine and allow it to warm up; nothing is a rush. Hitting the button on the machine starts the grinding of the beans. Many times, I'll watch the beans bounce and go into the grinder. Then as the water is pushed through the beans, I'll pause to smell the aroma of fresh-brewed espresso.

The small indigo blue cup, my favorite, is perfect for two shots of espresso. Slowly sipping the crema on top and then the coffee, the full range of flavors hit my tongue. With my coffee, I often walk outside and connect to the ground, observing whatever happens. Warm weather or cold, I will do this to sync up with the start of the day.

Imagine beginning a morning like that versus rushing out of bed, jumping into the shower, and slamming down a cup of coffee on your way out the door into traffic and work.

Keep in mind it doesn't have to be my specific actions; it can be whatever you want it to be, with the idea of being present and calm. Think about the contrast of a hurried beginning versus enjoying a quiet morning.

Reflection

Try doing one thing tomorrow morning to start your day off in a state of calm. It can be anything you like. Stay in the shower for an extra few minutes enjoying the hot water without urgency. Savor your coffee or breakfast. Watch the sunrise while being present in the moment.

Ritual 3: Ippuku

Ippuku means taking a breath or short break. In a fun twist of meaning that I explain later, it can even mean pausing for a smoke break.

We sometimes react to stressful situations without thinking. Our reactions come without much thought, often based on fear and insecurities. A quick reaction is rarely the most rational, appropriate, or even productive way to act. If we employ ippuku and pause, it allows us to respond rather than react. We can take in the situation and calmly decide the best course of action based on our values.

Let's take a common example: You're driving down the highway and someone cuts you off in traffic, nearly causing a wreck.

React: You get angry, perhaps honking the horn. They gesture back and you honk the horn again. Your anger heats up and you are frustrated for the remainder of the drive home.

With ippuku we respond instead of reacting.

Respond: You notice your initial anger reaction, then pause, take a breath, and reflect on the situation. No damage was done to either car and your trip home won't be noticeably delayed. You can recall times you've done the same thing accidentally and decide to give the other driver the benefit of the doubt. Perhaps they did the same thing, accidentally cutting you off.

Ippuku in Action   Years ago, when MRIs were new, I was a National Support Engineer for General Electric's medical division. It was supposed to be a glamourous promotion from working on the scanners in the hospitals and eventually it became such a job. Initially, it was a glorified call center operator trying to fix complex medical devices remotely without any remote tools or capabilities. These were the days of 14.4 kilobits per second modems, well before high-speed internet connections.

We would sit in a four-person cubicle space fielding calls from frustrated radiology technicians struggling with malfunctioning MRI scanners and anxious patients left waiting. One after another, the calls would come, and we'd do our best to get the machines scanning again.

During a particularly busy day I was on a long call with a hospital. When I finished, I noticed the list of waiting customers hadn't gone down at all. It had kept growing while no existing calls were leaving the queue. I turned to ask the other engineers near me if they noticed, and no one was there.

Standing up from my chair, I looked around, and there weren't any engineers at any of the desks. The team I was part of had a lot of smokers. For years, they could smoke at their desks, but as times changed, they had to move outside.

Eventually I noticed the entire team was outside taking a "smoke" break, even the ones who didn't smoke. The non-smokers, like me, got tired of handling the support lines while the smokers took breaks, so we all decided to become "smokers" and take a break together minus the cigarettes.

You should have seen the look on my wife's face that day when I told her I had decided to take up smoking. Of course I didn't really. What I did do was begin to incorporate more breaks into my day. Hour after hour and day after day of taking urgent calls for help from people who were upset and dealing with medical emergencies was taking an emotional toll. I didn't realize at the time, the "smoke breaks" were like employing the ippuku ritual of calm to help me respond rather than to react to the stress of my job.

Reflection

Take some time to notice your response to frustrations, injustices, or disappointing events. What are you feeling in these circumstances? Notice all of the feelings . . . frustration, anger, disappointment, betrayal, whatever it is.

Are there outside events impacting the way you feel about this one situation? Were you already tired and frustrated by something else that contributed to this being a bigger frustration than it really needs to be?

My personal hot button right now is being on the receiving end of poor customer service. I commit to being extra observant of my feelings and response in those situations. If you find yourself wanting to react, take a moment without acting and just breathe.

You'll find, in most cases, the urgency to respond goes away. Then there is an opportunity to apply thought, reason, patience, and grace to the situation. And please embrace only the small break part of ippuku; don't take up smoking.

Ritual 4: Mujo

Mujo, which means "impermanence," is about realizing that nothing is permanent, including how we feel about something frustrating. It blends with an attitude of Ki ni shimasen, which literally translated means "I don't care," in the sense of not letting something bother you.

Often, our reaction (Ritual 2) is to take things personally. When someone does something we don't like, we interpret this as a personal affront. Being cutoff in traffic becomes a personal attack or insult. Is the boss short with us? Our minds can conjure all sorts of awful scenarios. How could they treat me this way?! Don't they think I'm doing a good job? I might get fired!

Withholding or delaying judgment in those circumstances is one of the most effective ways to remain calm and reduce the noise of irritation in our lives. More often than not, it isn't intentionally directed at you at all. Usually, it's the other person's issue they're dealing with in their own lives. Many people are doing the best they can. When we embrace the ritual of Mujo we learn not to interpret actions as a personal attack.

Here's an example from my own life. Not long ago, I was short with my wife when she asked me a question. Instead of getting angry, she quietly and without judgment asked me if everything was alright.

I told her it was and wondered why she asked. She explained I had answered her in a sharp and almost angry tone. That wasn't my intention. Distracted, my sharp answer was an expression of frustration at myself for trying to do too many things simultaneously.

By delaying judgment, she didn't jump to the conclusion that could quickly have escalated the issue. Her question helped me realize I wasn't being present in anything I was doing. It helped me slow down, focus on one thing, and allow my energy to even out. Framing something as non-personal allows you to acknowledge it as happening without needing to respond.

I used to have a long commute. One trip in particular was a chance for me to apply a Mujo practice. Arriving home that day, every muscle in my body was tight. My neck felt like it would snap if I moved too far to the right or left. Being nearly wrecked by a speeding car with one of those COEXIST bumper stickers was only one frustrating experience in my 90-minute commute home.

Sitting in the car before going into the house, I spent some time praying and breathing, releasing anger, frustration, and negative energy. It was a practice I had developed years before.

When I came home angry or frustrated, I realized that energy was projected into the house for my wife and children. All they wanted was some love and attention from dad. They didn't need the negative energy.

It would have been better if I had not gotten angry or frustrated from work or traffic to begin with, but as with most things, the change started small.

My small beginning was ensuring love and positive energy were projected into the home upon my arrival. When we commit to changing our attitudes, negative emotions, or toxic behaviors, we begin a journey of self-healing. This process not only benefits us individually but also has a ripple effect on the world around us. As we grow and improve, our positive changes influence our family, friends, and even casual acquaintances.

By embracing the impermanence of even a tough commute and adopting a Ki ni shimasen (I don't care) attitude, I prepared myself to be present for my family. This approach helped me heal a small part of the world around me by healing myself. Becoming whole in this area of life was serving my family.

It's a big job healing the world—too big for us alone. As we grow into our Ikigai, we are healing ourselves and, by extension, bringing healing to a small part of the world. Embracing the impermanence of our existence and not caring about things we cannot change multiplies that healing power.

Reflection

Build on what you learned in Ritual 2, by going beyond noticing your response to frustrations, injustices, or disappointing events to eliminating judgment altogether. Recall the meaning of Mujo, remembering that nothing is permanent, including how we feel about something frustrating. Embrace Ki ni shimasen, I don't care, and see how different your day goes.

Ritual 5: Kanasha

"If the only prayer you said in your whole life were, 'thank you,' that would suffice."

—Meister Eckhart

Kanasha means gratitude. A practice of gratitude focuses our minds on the good things in our lives. Our brains tend to find what we are looking for or expecting. If we are looking for problems or bad news we tend to notice those things in our lives. Do that often enough and it seems like we are experiencing nothing but problems and receiving a lot of bad news.

The opposite is also true. When we look for things to be grateful for, we notice the positive events in our lives. Let's look at five simple ways to incorporate gratitude into your life.

1. Start each day with one minute of gratitude reflection. Nothing complicated; think of three things you are grateful for today.
2. When you're having a hard day make a gratitude list. Take a moment to recall the good things in your life and release the bad.
3. Respond with gratitude. In prior rituals, we learned to notice our reactions and release judgment. These combine well with Ritual 4, Mujo. When we experience something frustrating, become aware of our reaction, release judgment, and let our response be gratitude.
4. When you face a major change, be grateful for it. Look for the learning that could come as a result.
5. Look at what you have and not what you don't. It is easy to see people around us who have more and yet an average person living a middle-class life has more riches than kings of old. A friend of mine would answer a "how are you?" greeting with "better than most." She was right. We are healthier, face fewer catastrophes, and live longer today than any generation before us.

A final though on Kanasha. When you are living your Ikigai, simply being your authentic self becomes a profound act of giving thanks.

Reflection

Begin your Kanasha with something small. As you start your quiet morning, take a moment and list three things you are grateful for. If three feels like too much, come up with one. Spend a moment in thankful meditation on your Kanasha list and the blessings the content represents.

Ritual 6: Yasuragi

Yasuragi means tranquility and represents inner peace that comes from reducing sources of stress. Achieving more moments of inner peace can be accomplished by either removing the sources of stress or developing practices and habits that support you in dealing with stress.

Smiling   Something as simple as smiling can be one of these practices. Who hasn't seen someone under stress and could tell by the look on their face? Smiling not only helps to keep us from looking tired, worn out, and overwhelmed, it can truly help reduce stress-related hormones, increasing the mood-boosting ones instead.

It is almost impossible to remain stressed while smiling. The next time you feel stressed, smile; you'll be surprised by the difference it can make.

In addition to smiling, being present is a powerful stress reducer. Consciously decide to appreciate and experience today. Soak in as many of the sights, sounds, smells, feelings, and experiences of today as you can. Pick one thing to observe and notice how different you feel.

Your phone, social media, and email all lead to interrupted thoughts and fragmented days. We are never present for very long before something interrupts. Disconnecting, even for a short time, allows your brain to rest, reset, and focus. Stress levels drop when we are rested and focused.

Reframing   Reframing is a potent technique for cultivating inner peace by transforming our perception of experiences. I've made a simple yet profound change in my life: replacing the word "stress" with "excitement." When I have a lot going on, even good things, I used to say, "I have a lot of stress." Now, I reframe it by saying, "I have a lot of excitement in my life."

Importantly, the feeling itself hasn't changed—what's different is how I label and perceive it. It's amazing how this simple reframe can alter my entire outlook. As an example, when those familiar sensations come up before an upcoming vacation, instead of labeling them as "stress," I now recognize and name them as "excitement" for the trip.

Exercise   Exercising is another effective way to reduce stress. I often joke that running keeps me married. Not only does it get me out of the house to give my wife some time to herself, it is almost impossible to remain stressed after a nice, long run. I'm always in a better mood after a run, and it isn't just mental. Exercise releases mood-boosting hormones and brain chemicals.

Removing or avoiding stress-producing activities is another way to embrace Yasuragi. For me, traffic is a frustrating and stress-inducing experience. When possible, I arrange my drives to avoid high-volume traffic times. Look for any opportunity to make adjustments to avoid those things that cause you stress, frustration, or worry.

One final thought on stress. When you are engaged in your Ikigai, you express your essence and purpose. There is no greater opportunity to reduce stress than while doing that.

Reflection

To embrace Yasuragi in your life, consider the Kaizen practice of doing one small thing. Drawing inspiration from the examples above, identify and remove one small stress-causing activity from your day or add one brief, stress-reducing practice to your routine. Notice how this tiny shift affects your sense of inner peace over the next few days.

Ritual 7: Isshin Furan

Isshin Furan represents "single-minded concentration" or "absolute focus." Many practices help you be here in the moment and present in your life. One to add to your ritual toolkit is the idea of monotasking or single focus.

For years people have been convinced that multitasking was a great way to get more done in the same amount of time. In my own coaching and consulting, I found my clients underperformed when trying to multitask versus a single focus effort. I encouraged them to "monotask" by making a jokingly reference to singularly focused effort. This was decades ago, and for all I know, I coined the term. Many studies have since confirmed my observation about multitasking was correct.

Multitasking isn't doing many things at once. It is still single processing with multiple tiny disruptions and decisions being made. Each stop and each task switch add to cognitive load and ultimately slows down completion of each task.

Multitasking wears us out mentally. We are switching and making many timing decisions in addition to task switching decisions that the resulting mental exhaustion increases the likelihood of making mistakes.

The cognitive drain also means we have less capacity to deal with complex ideas or make in-depth analysis. This adds to the attention gap we often blame on social media. The frenetic pace needed to multitask also contributes to poorly thought-out responses and decisions. Though discredited in numerous studies, the practice continues.

Monotasking is the new multitasking. Being able to focus and immerse ourselves in one thing is the productivity breakthrough we hoped would come from multitasking. It also allows us to be more present and focused, supporting our Ikigai reflections. The challenge, of course, is that our systems, our world, sometimes drive us to the multitasking mode without our even realizing it.

While the example I use is monotasking, the ritual of Isshin Furan goes far deeper than simply doing one task at a time. It represents absolute focus and commitment. Ikigai in its purest state is the singular focus and mission of expressing who we are and why we are here in harmony with whatever we are doing.

While writing this book I employed Isshin Furan. I paused all my other endeavors to focus my creative energies on sharing Ikigai in the most helpful, supportive, and meaningful way possible. There were 500 other things my mind wanted to think about, and yet if I had paid attention to them, I wouldn't have been focused on any of them, least of all this book.

Any new idea I came up with or new opportunity I was offered, I'd note so it could be recalled later and then I went back to my book.

It is akin to what I did while working in a highly demanding corporate executive role to be present for my family. Something would come up on a Friday afternoon and even if I couldn't work on it over the weekend, it would take my focus away from my weekend activities.

Applying Isshin Furan, I began to note whatever the issue was in an email and send it to myself as a reminder to handle on Monday. Sometimes I'd even put it in a calendar entry if I needed uninterrupted time to work on it.

With that taken care of, I didn't have to "remember" it all weekend or work on it. I knew it was taken care of and could be addressed with my full attention on Monday. In the meantime, I placed my full attention on what I was doing or experiencing on the weekend, like my kid's soccer game. I was watching them play rather than pondering work.

Isshin Furan frees you to be focused, present, and more effective in whatever you are doing.

Reflection

When was the last time you let yourself focus singly on doing or thinking about only one thing? You should try it even today. Monotasking is the new, new thing.

The Seven Ritual Process

Now that you've read all seven rituals, remember, everything starts small. There is no right or wrong way to explore these practices.

1. Kaizen (small change).
2. Shizuka (quiet).

3. Ippuku (pause, take a moment).
4. Mujo (delay judgment).
5. Kanasha (gratitude).
6. Yasuragi (inner peace).
7. Isshin Furan (singular focus).

One easy way to get started is to read each of the rituals again in order. Then return to the first ritual and focus on the learning and reflection for a day.

The next day go to the second ritual and do the same until you've gone seven days and touched on each ritual. One small step is all you need to get started. Once you get going, repeat the process for several weeks or pick one to focus on for an entire week. As with everything Kaizen, give yourself permission to start small and even "terrible." No pressure, just presence.

In the next chapter, we'll dive deeper into the importance of getting the noise down through a story that illustrates the profound impact reducing the noise can have on every part of your life.

5

From Chaos to Calm

HERE IS AN example of the importance of getting the noise down and how it can lead to setting up that virtuous cycle I talked about in prior chapters. The goal, as the chapter title suggests, is to move from chaos into calm.

The Metavante Challenge

After 10 years with GE, I was recruited to a company called Metavante, where I was the vice president of Technology Services. What I didn't know when I took that job is there had been five people in the role of vice president of Technology Services in the prior seven years.

It didn't take me very long to figure out why. I spent most of my day getting yelled at because the systems were failing. Every day, clients were being handled inappropriately and situations were going wrong. As a result, there were all these customer issues that were escalated to me.

I'd spend the entire day getting yelled at for all the stuff that had happened wrong the day before or the day before that or weeks before that with barely time to do anything else.

Pager Problem

To give you an idea of the level of distraction, after I'd been there for just a month, my boss let me know that I had gone over my limit on my pager, that I'd received too many pages. This is back when we still wore pagers. Cell phones were around; we just didn't use them very often because they were expensive, and prior to smartphones texting wasn't as big a thing.

I asked, "Well, how many pages do I get per month before we have an overage charge?" He said, "1500," and that he wanted me to cut down on the number of pages I received. I took the pager off my belt, set it on his desk, and said, "Here, you can have it back. I don't want to be paged that many times."

Imagine the distraction of 1,500 pages or, if you make it in the equivalent of today's thinking, 1,500 text messages throughout the month. My team was escalating every single event to me, even routine issues.

Every ticket that was opened, closed, or updated—everything that happened—was escalated to me. On top of that, I had all the real escalations which were the things that should be handled by the vice president. There were no metrics, no way of understanding what was going on, just the feeling of getting our heads kicked in every single day.

Measures and Metrics

To reduce the noise, I had to better understand the current condition. Applying the first ritual of calm, Kaizen, I started small by trying to establish some level of measurement to understand what was happening. Again, there were no measurements in place. The only thing I could determine was how many times issues got escalated to me, the vice president. That became my first measure.

It was a small measure, and something I could develop and grow over time. It also didn't require a metrics team or other departments to create. This kept it easy and eliminated conflicts that could come from those other departments. Recall from the previous chapter that when faced with a significant change in our lives, fear kicks in. Keeping the metric simple and under my control eliminated the possibility of generating fear in the other teams.

Breaking it down, I determined there were about 20 customer escalations a month. I knew from experience those 20 formal escalations represented probably hundreds of other issues.

Think about the number of workdays you typically get in a month. It's around 20. Which meant I was involved in all-day escalations every workday while a new issue was being ignored and becoming the next escalation.

That is a vicious cycle of noise, distraction, and energy drain that led to more problems and the cycle repeating. It created chaos.

An Old Marine Trick

I began the noise reduction effort by applying Isshin Furan, a single focus, doing a deeper dive into understanding the reasons for the escalations themselves. My research showed a number of escalations were for vendor issues, both before I arrived and since I joined as vice president.

We were operating the networks for large banks and other financial institutions. An ATM cash machine or a bank teller system might go down and the bank would call into our Network Operations Center (NOC).

If it couldn't be fixed remotely, and almost nothing could be fixed remotely at the time, our engineers would dispatch a vendor.

If this happened during the day, engineers on that shift would dispatch the vendor, but the vendor might not get back to us or go out to the site right away. When the evening and overnight teams came in they didn't know to follow up and make sure the vendor addressed the customer's problem.

The following morning the day shift team would assume the issue had been taken care of and there would be no follow-up. As a result, it might be three or four days later, and the vendor still hadn't gone to the bank. That's when I would get my escalation. So, I implemented something very simple from my Marine Corps days where we had a turnover log.

Every day the technical team leaders wrote in a green binder what had happened, what was still pending, and what next steps were. The Non-Commissioned Officer in Charge (NCO-IC) would sign the log and the NCO-IC taking over would read the entry and sign that they had read it. A simple accountability practice.

I instituted that plan in the NOC at Metavante. About 3 p.m., as the evening shift manager was coming on, I called a quick meeting with both day and evening managers.

Placing an archive quality journal on the table with a thud for emphasis, I said to the day shift manager, "You're going to write in this what happened today and what's still pending."

Motioning to the evening manager, I said, "You are going to read and sign the log, acknowledging that you've read it. Tonight, when the midnight shift manager comes in, you'll brief them on the situation, write it in the log, and both of you will sign it, confirming that you've written it and they've read it."

The Virtuous Cycle Begins

As noted earlier, in a typical month, there are about 20 working days. Prior to implementing this simple turnover log, I was facing escalations every single day, leaving no time to focus on anything else. The constant noise and churn made it clear why my five predecessors had struggled in this role, ultimately failing.

By embracing the gift of small beginnings, that one small change immediately reduced escalations by about four in a month. Now with four fewer escalations, I've got some time to think, where I'm not getting beaten up by a customer or one of our internal teams. Even if it was only four days, those were four I didn't have previously.

Yasuragi as a ritual of calm represents inner peace. It comes from reducing sources of stress. Achieving more moments of inner peace can be accomplished by either removing the sources of stress or developing practices and habits that support you in dealing deal with stress.

In this case, eliminating those vendor escalations did both. It reduced the stress of the all-day meetings and customers complaints as well as provided the team with a mechanism to own the support issues and deal with them more effectively. Before the NOC representatives felt powerless; now, they were learning there were ways to make their lives and work better.

Now with four days to play with, I could start looking at what's the next thing and the next. Little by little, I begin investing those four days in getting the noise down even more.

As more issues were resolved, I reinvested whatever time was saved on the next level of noise reduction. Within six months, I had it down to zero escalations to the vice president of Technology Services . . . me.

The virtuous cycle was starting to spin. Like a flywheel that moves slowly at first, the more momentum you get the faster it goes.

Simplify, Simplify, Simplify

With the virtuous cycle in motion and no escalations coming to me, I began attacking other issues like our internal communications. Remember the 1,500 pages I was receiving? The team had no idea what a formal escalation process looked like. Rather than add noise by trying to implement something advanced with people who had never been trusted to make decisions, I came up with a simple protocol.

"If it is going to get Dave (me) yelled at, you should page me," were my instructions. Simple straightforward and highly effective. If something was going bad, they would page me. If a customer was getting upset, again it was probably eventually going to get me yelled at. I wanted to be able to help sooner rather than later.

This was an application of Ippuku—taking a breath or short break before acting. We often react to stressful situations without thinking. Our reactions come without much thought, often based on fear and insecurities.

This team was under constant pressure and stress. Fear drove them to react by escalating everything to the vice president. Employing Ippuku and pausing allowed them to think rather than react. When we do that, we can take in the situation and calmly decide the best course of action based on our values.

I was also creating a culture of delaying judgment, which is the fourth ritual of calm. Ki ni shimasen, which literally translated means "I don't care" in the sense of not letting something bother you.

The team was given this simple protocol for escalation. If for any reason something should have been escalated but wasn't we wouldn't get upset or "care." We would analyze it. Applying Kaizen we would then make small improvements to the process based on the learning. There was never any condemnation or judgment from me on how they handled anything. We would always embrace every issue as an opportunity to learn and improve.

I added in a few periodic updates on open issues and that was it. Fewer than 8 pages a day, down from 50.

Beginning the Transformation

Eventually the flywheel was spinning fast enough that we could reinvent our entire service offering. When I took over, the NOC was a 95% reactive environment where things broke, customers called, and the engineers tried to fix them. By getting the noise down and reinvesting the time, money, and focus capacity, we were able to create a 98% proactive service. We created technology and systems that detected or predicted problems, and either repaired or prevented them before the customer even knew about it.

We got so good at preventing issues and ensuring the customer's system never failed that we had to redo our marketing. Customers started questioning the value of paying for our service contracts since their systems were running smoothly without any breakdowns. A good problem to have. When we explained the value of preventing issues rather than "fixing" them, they were happy to pay for our service.

With all the time saved, the support engineers went from taking phone calls and paging me all the time to doing analysis and planning as value-added services. They helped customers design and implement better technology solutions. Job satisfaction soared.

We celebrated victories and demonstrated Kanasha, the fifth ritual of gratitude on a regular basis. My department went from losing money and a target to being outsourced to making hundreds of millions of dollars and securing all those jobs. Those employees embraced Kanasha as well, and their job performance rose in tandem with their job satisfaction.

As the systems improved, we introduced Shizuka, the second ritual of calm, which focuses on quiet and stillness. No longer in a state of constant urgency, the team could start their workday at a more relaxed pace, taking the time to connect with their colleagues and center themselves. Throughout the day, there were opportunities for breaks and leisurely lunches, a stark contrast to the early days when most people didn't even take a lunch break. This newfound time allowed team members to get to know each other better and foster a sense of camaraderie.

All by starting with getting the noise level down.

Personal Applications of Noise Reduction

The noise reduction wasn't limited to only work. By cutting out the off-hour pages, I was more present at home. My sleep wasn't interrupted, and without the urgency of morning escalation meetings I could begin my morning quietly applying Shizuka. This enabled greater energy and focus to drive the improvements.

Because I was on call and saving so much money on my "pager" bill, I talked my boss into getting me a cell phone. This freed me up to attend all my kids' school events, knowing I could easily communicate with my team in an emergency.

When I accepted that job, I made the decision to have a longer commute rather than disrupt my family's life with a move. By avoiding the need for a new house, the challenge of making new friends, and the adjustment to a new school for my children, I felt that a longer drive was a worthwhile trade-off. In this case I applied Yasuragi and reduced stress for my family.

The downside was I was home later. As soon as I hit the door the kids wanted my attention, which of course was great. However, this left little time for my wife and me to catch up or for her to brief me on any important matters the kids might need to discuss with me. This added a certain amount of stress to my life and my relationship with my wife.

To remove this stress, I began using my new cell phone. I'd call and talk to her all the way home. It gave us a chance to connect without the kids interrupting as well as allow me time to decompress. Once I arrived home, I was able to be all in with the kids while still maintaining a strong connection with my wife.

This virtuous cycle of improved work life and home life kept paying dividends. I had plenty of energy and time for investing in the next new thing at work, which helped my career. With less stress at work, I had more time and energy for my family. With promotions came more money that I could invest in the family and our future.

The better sleep I was getting also led to having the "What would you do if you were done" dream, which of course led to uncovering my Ikigai.

Applying the Seven Rituals

The seven rituals of calm are designed to get the flywheel of positive change spinning in your life. By applying these rituals, you can create capacity in various forms: focus, energy, time, and even money. Often, stress-induced behaviors can burn through our resources, both emotional and financial. For example, people who come home stressed out from work or a tough commute may spend money on things to help them relax, rather than cultivating a calm mindset during their journey home.

If you look closely at the Metavante example, you will see all seven rituals of calm applied in some form. From the simple act of creating a turnover log (Kaizen and Shizuka) to celebrating victories openly (Kanasha), each ritual played a role in reducing noise. The flywheel started spinning, and the results were increased job satisfaction, improved customer relationships, and a more profitable department. The benefits of the rituals extended far beyond work to life at home.

Instead of exhausted and burnt out from a tough day at work, I had more energy and focus when I arrived home. I was present for my family and had the capacity to invest time and energy in things that brought me joy and fulfillment.

If you haven't started incorporating the seven rituals into your life, I encourage you to revisit them today and, as always, start small. Even something as simple as writing a three-item gratitude list or starting your morning in a state of calm can set the virtuous cycle in motion.

Remember, the examples given here represent only the beginning of the good that can come from reducing noise in your life. As you continue to apply the seven rituals of calm, you'll find yourself creating more capacity for the things that truly matter to you. In the next chapter, we'll explore some more ways to keep the flywheel spinning and maintain the positive momentum you've created.

6

Glimpses of Ikigai

THE FIRST INVITATION of Ikigai is getting the noise down, and the reason to get the noise down is so you can hear that still, small voice of purpose in your life. In the example I gave you with Metavante in the last chapter, the noise level was outrageous in every aspect of my life: at work, home, my commute, my hobbies, everything.

The idea behind the seven rituals is to get you started on getting the noise down and taking advantage of those quiet moments to hear that still-small voice of purpose. Here's an example of how reinvesting time from noise reduction enabled me to hear my quiet voice of purpose.

Hidden Treasure

The clues to your purpose have been present throughout your life. Often, we're too busy following the default path to notice them.

Or there's so much noise in our lives that we can't hear it. Making space for quiet reflection is how we hear that still, small voice.

Because I've invested time in getting the noise down, I have capacity to reinvest in myself. I have that flywheel moving. At the end of each year, I make time for quiet reflection and journaling. During one of those periods of reflection, a particular memory resurfaced—what I'll call an achievement story. Reflecting on your achievement stories is one of the best ways to uncover clues to our purpose. I'll talk more about that in a bit.

59

This memory was so enjoyable to recall, I felt compelled to write about it. As is often the case when I write about things, I uncovered a deeper truth—something that has been part of my Ikigai my whole life. There are often hidden treasures of insight in a childhood memory.

The fascinating thing is how this achievement reflection reignited a long-hidden passion in the last year or so, ultimately leading me to write this book. I'm going to share that story with you, and then at the end, I'll talk more about the value of spending time in quiet.

Jumping the Stairs

Reaching the fourth step would require speed, which meant running, and running was forbidden. Re-entry into the gothic building that was my elementary school was supposed to be quiet and orderly. No one in my class had yet achieved the jump to the fourth step. My last attempt had grazed it but not held.

Kids walking single file, holding the railing, gave me the opening to jump in the middle of the staircase. Leaning back slowly and then lunging forward, I ran toward my target.

"Made it," I whispered, barely able to contain the joy of accomplishing what no one else had done before.

"David," came a voice from down the stairs. It was my teacher, Mrs. Huff. Going back down those four steps was slower and less enthusiastic than had been the historic trip up. I knew I was in trouble. Mrs. Huff put her arm around my shoulder, something she always did when she wanted to talk directly to someone.

"I have some news for you. You won the governor's essay award. I'm going to announce it to the class and wanted to tell you first." She shook my hand and said, "Congratulations. Go on upstairs. I'll be there in a few minutes."

"Oh, and this time, walk." We both smiled.

Months before, we'd been assigned to write about our home state of Indiana. Every elementary kid in the state was required to write an essay. We had an old set of encyclopedias at home. I dug them out and began writing. It seemed an enormous task at the time. Relief was all I felt when I turned in the three-page essay.

The relief was short-lived when Mrs. Huff returned it to me the next day, saying it wasn't what the assignment asked for and I needed to do it again. I turned in the revised essay twice more, but it was returned to me both times.

"It's not supposed to be facts from the encyclopedia David; it's supposed to be your story of Indiana." What story? How was I supposed to tell my story? I didn't have a story.

Little did I know, but I had a story to tell—quite a good story, as it turned out. At the prompting of my grandmother, I told the story of our family trip to Michigan to visit relatives. It required us to drive nearly the length of Indiana from bottom to top and back again on mostly country roads.

It was quite the adventure before interstate highways and cell phones. If you came upon a gas station, you bought gas because if you ran out, there might not be another station (or person) around for dozens of miles. If you got a flat, there was no one to call. I shared all of it and then some: five total pages, two more than the minimum requirement.

"Much better," said Mrs. Huff of this version, and it wasn't mentioned again until that day on the stairs. I had no idea there was even a contest. It was probably in the instructions. As you may have guessed, I didn't read them carefully in the first place, or I wouldn't have had to repeat the assignment three times before getting it right.

Our governor at the time was a military hero who had written his story of escape from a Japanese POW camp in World War II. Each grade had an essay contest winner who received an autographed copy of his book. I still have mine and the black and white photo of the ceremony cut from the newspaper.

When we were back in our classroom, Mrs. Huff shared the news, and the class erupted with applause, especially at my reading table. My friend Peter slapped me on the back and said, "You won, and you're in the second reading group!"

We both were in the second reading group. Third grade was when they began to divide us academically, and we in the second group weren't as "good" as the first. I became a hero to the others in the second reading group. After all, no one in the first reading group had won anything.

Looking back, we all saw ourselves differently in the second reading group from then on. I began writing more stories in earnest, even when they weren't assigned.

Something new came to me as I wrote about this memory. I've never understood this event the way I understand it now. This was an early glimpse of my Ikigai. I realize now, as early as nine years old, I loved telling stories and inspiring people to believe in themselves. Even as I retell it, I can feel the joy I felt back then.

Reflecting on Your Achievement Stories

What is an early achievement story in your life? Achievement, in this case, is a moment of success, victory, pride, growth, or satisfaction. Revisit it. Sit with this memory for a while.

- What did you do, feel, or see?
- Why is it an achievement story?
- Are there any early glimpses of Ikigai in it for you?

Case Study: Meet Tom

Here's a story of someone who had a great deal of noise in his life and was a mess in every part of it.

Tom[1] sought me out because his life wasn't what he wanted it to be despite having seemingly everything anyone could want. He was a 54-year-old married father of three, an executive at a well-known company, with a beautiful home and all that.

Tom . . .

- Hated his job.
- Needed to lose weight.
- Loved his wife though the relationship had grown stale.
- Was distant from his children, especially the oldest about to leave for college.

He had a fitness coach, a nutrition coach, a life coach, and a relationship coach and still wasn't where he wanted to be. Having tried countless self-help books and methods, he found my work on Ikigai and reached out.

The interesting thing about Tom was none of those coaches could help him fill the gaps in his life or solve his issues.

He later confessed that he couldn't imagine how Ikigai could help where all these other coaches had failed. Though skeptical, Tom reached out to me anyway.

Starting the Noise Reduction

We started with the Three Invitations of Ikigai, especially the first invitation, getting the noise down. The cacophony in Tom's life was deafening.

For Tom much of the noise was being generated by the voices in his head. We get layers and layers and layers of things built on us of what we should do and have to do and ought to do. Then for Tom there was the noise of a growing sense of mortality. We all reach that point where we understand that there's a time limit. For Tom, his kids were growing up, and as is often the case you start to see some of the things in yourself that you haven't dealt with surfacing in your children.

Increasing the urgency was his oldest daughter heading off to college. He didn't feel like he was as close to her as he wanted to be, and time was running out for that as well.

That's what was going on with Tom. He felt like he needed more. What do you do when you've reached the point where you have everything you thought you wanted, it's not enough, and there's nothing more?

The first step for Tom was getting the noise level down in his life. Tom had a perfect lawn and felt pressure to spend most of his weekends mowing or caring for the lawn. Not only was he putting in a significant amount of time on the lawn, but he was also exhausted and unavailable for his family afterward. He was so tired he preferred to sit in his chair snacking and watching television.

We reprioritized Tom's time and expectations so that he only needed to spend time on the lawn every other weekend. The lawn could still look nice and now he could invest the other weekend in his family.

It also came up that he did the lawncare work because his children didn't like doing it. Part of the reason they didn't like doing it was because Tom wanted everything exactly right and, as we all know, kids rarely do everything "right" in the sense of what experienced adults would do.

Tom lowered his expectations and invited his kids to help. His son started working with him and enjoyed the less pressured environment. Working in the yard together eventually became a bonding experience for Tom and his son.

Tom had every bit of fitness equipment you could imagine. None of it got used. I introduced him to Kaizen and suggested he do something small to start with rather than an overwhelming fitness program. It had to be something bite-sized that he would commit to doing daily. We decided on walking for no more than 15 minutes.

As soon as he arrived home from work, he would go for a walk. This had multiple benefits. It allowed him to move his body after a long commute, providing exercise and stress relief. When he finished, he was more relaxed and present for his family.

His habit upon arriving home had been to grab a high-calorie snack. With his walk, the snack time was now filled with movement and occupied his mind, so he didn't crave a snack.

By now you see where this is going. The movement combined with his eliminating empty calorie snacking resulted in losing a little weight. Over time he began walking longer, and eventually Evelynn, his wife, started joining him.

Tom had shared with me that he really wanted to travel and there was no travel in their life. His wife always protested whenever the idea of traveling came up. I suggested he talk with her about it on one of their relaxed walks.

Several weeks went by and he finally got the courage to ask why she didn't want to travel. She was terrified that he wanted her to go whitewater rafting or parachute into the Amazonian jungle and hack their way back out. Don't laugh, our minds can conjure up all kinds of scary scenarios.

Tom was always talking about wanting to do exciting things, so Evelyn assumed he wanted to go on exotic and dangerous vacations. It turned out he didn't want to camp on safari in a tent and risk being eaten by lions. He wanted to experience unique places, places that they hadn't seen before. He and Evelyn hadn't been to France. Something new and exciting might mean visiting the Eiffel Tower in Paris.

Expressing what each needed, they identified some places where they could both have what they were looking for. A bit of adventure without big risk. The flywheel of the virtuous cycle was starting to move. Noise reduction continued to provide time, focus, and energy for Tom to reinvest. This enabled us in our coaching sessions to focus on the Second Invitation of Ikigai, uncovering purpose.

Transformative Power of Purpose

I wish I could show you Tom's face when his purpose finally became clear to him. It was like a lifetime of confusion and disappointment had been lifted. I'll share more of uncovering Tom's purpose when we explore the Second Invitation of Ikigai in full. What is important to know now is that having both an understanding of his purpose and the emotional energy from noise reduction, Tom was able to have a conversation with his boss.

He shared his purpose and desire to find ways to live into it at work. In recent years his role had morphed into a lot of meetings and bureaucratic stuff. He wanted to have a closer impact on the world as a whole and people in general.

The sensational thing was his boss thought it was great that he wanted to align his purpose to his work. He even thought of some things they could adjust right away. Together they began to reorient Tom's job focus. He didn't change jobs or accountabilities in terms of what department he ran. Instead, he spent more of his time on the areas that he was most interested in. Right away his work life was noticeably better.

He didn't lose any weight with the fitness coach, but he lost 10 pounds through nothing more than getting the noise down. The future no longer came with a sense of foreboding. Now there was a sense of opportunity to do things that he wanted to do.

Before, Tom envisioned his window for travel shrinking and his wife's resistance as a barrier. Reorienting his time and focus enabled him to plan travel, and his wife was on board. The 20 to 30 years of remaining life didn't seem as a negative in that sense.

Finally, Tom was more present for his entire family. When he was "present" before, as in physically there, he was the opposite of consciously present. With so much weighing on him and bothering him, he really wasn't very present, and that was part of the problem with his daughter.

By getting the noise level down and clearing out some of the things, Tom was able to be present in every way with his family.

With his daughter, instead of feeling foreboding about her going off to college, there was an openness to share the experience with her, spending specific time with just her before she left.

Tom's diet improved dramatically. Again, I'm not a nutrition coach, but I do understand stress eating, and using Kaizen helped him eliminate that. Tom said he lost 10 pounds right away in the time we were working together. The secret is getting the noise level down and then uncovering that purpose.

You don't find your purpose. It's not a thing you've got to find because it's there all along. It is a process of uncovering.

Think about children at play. My granddaughter loves to skip, and I love watching her skip because when she is skipping, she is happy. She's being a kid, and in being a kid, she is expressing everything she is meant to be in that moment. She doesn't need to find herself. That's what living your Ikigai is all about. That first step, or skip, is to get the noise down.

The Essential First Step

It should be apparent by now why getting the noise down is so vital and why it is the first invitation of Ikigai. You've got some background on applying it. Take a moment right now and revisit the seven rituals of calm.

1. Kaizen (small change).
2. Shizuka (quiet).
3. Ippuku (pause, take a moment).
4. Mujo (delay judgment).

5. Kanasha (gratitude).
6. Yasuragi (inner peace).
7. Isshin Furan (singular focus).

Getting the noise down is the essential first step to experiencing all the incredible possibilities, profound wisdom, and life-changing benefits that come with uncovering your Ikigai. Now that you are incorporating them into your everyday life you are ready for the Second Invitation of Ikigai . . . uncovering your purpose, which we explore next.

7

Ikiverse

THE NATURE OF our lives is made real by the language we use. Most of us operate in the default language in life. Default means to assume a preset value or take a preselected action, unless otherwise instructed. Returning unintentionally to an original position, basically to do what we've always done. That is how most of us live the first half of our lives, on the default autopilot.

There's a second definition for default that takes on more significance as we enter the second half of life where autopilot doesn't work anymore. In that definition default means to deceive, to cheat, to put wrong, to lead astray, to cause to be mistaken. To conceal a state of privation or deprivation in which things, that are essential for human well-being are scarce—lacking.

We hit a point in life where we are being deceived, cheated, and led astray by the default language. It is the use of this language that eventually covers up our Ikigai. The life we were meant to live, the one we were created for is obscured from view.

What is left is a state of deprivation, scarcity, and lack. Default language leads to disappointment and a lack of meaning and burnout. Somewhere along the way, we just begin shutting down parts of ourselves to be able to function in this default space. When we aren't living the integrated life of Ikigai we become disintegrated.

If the default language is about disintegration, the language of purpose is about possibility, opportunity, and integration. Integration means the act of putting together parts or elements and combining them, giving them meaning and making them whole.

When have you felt integrated in your life: sound, whole, complete? An integrated life is expressing who you are at your deepest levels. The you before the disappointments, before expectations, before pressures, before all the things life throws at us.

Then living out that essence by utilizing your gifts, your talents, your passions, and your calling. Being you and living out the reason you were created in the first place. All in harmony with whatever you are doing. An integrated self. Now I want to share with you a vision for what that life looks like.

The Ikigai Nexus

There is a misconception that Ikigai is your purpose. As we explore a deeper understanding, it will become clear that Ikigai is what enables you to live out your purpose and express it as your truest self.

In Chapter 1, I introduced the Ikigai Nexus (see Figure 7.1) demonstrating the connection and interdependencies between the elements of Ikigai.

Figure 7.1   The Ikigai Nexus.

To live out our Ikigai we've got to know who we are and why we are here and then find ways to express that in harmony with whatever we do. That is a big task! It's like being told you must run a marathon before you've even run a mile. Maybe before you've even bought the shoes.

Have no fear, in the spirit of Kaizen there is a small, simple, and incremental way to achieve all of that and more.

You'll notice Purpose is positioned at the top of the nexus. *That is intentional, because if we can get a working understanding of our purpose,* we can begin the process of uncovering our essence and find ways to express both our purpose and essence in every part of our lives.

If you can ask yourself questions, you can uncover your purpose, even if you have no idea what you are called to do today. Let's ask a couple right now.

- What is one small thing we could do to better understand our purpose?
- How might having a simple way to express our purpose support us in living our Ikigai?

Imagine if you had an easy way to both understand and express your purpose. Having a defined purpose, we can begin to engage in experiments and tests that give us a deeper understanding of what is meaningful in our lives. We could refine our understanding of our purpose and calling.

There's an old saying that applies, "If you can't explain it simply, you don't understand it well enough."[1] If we could simply understand and express our purpose, we can enlist the support of others. We can begin to refine our understanding of what our purpose is. That then helps us understand ourselves better and gives us opportunities to practice being our true selves.

I have such a way, and later in this chapter I will explain how through a few small steps you can have yours.

The Pareto Ikigai Principle. Revisiting the 80/20 Rule

Most people are familiar with the 80/20 rule or the Pareto Principle first observed by economist Vilfredo Pareto in 1896 and popularized by management consultant Richard Koch. Though widely known, few people actually understand it. The 80/20 rule simply states that a small percentage of our time produces the majority of the benefits in our lives.

The 80/20 rule is often applied in business where it's obvious that 80% of the work that's done is non-value add or waste. As someone who spent three decades leading Lean Six Sigma and process improvement transformations, I can tell you that it's probably generous to say that only 80% of the work is waste. I repeatedly found, even in highly successful and well-regarded companies, that 90–95% of what was being done had no value.

A small number of experiences, inputs, or effort lead to a majority of the positive results, or rewards. While it's common to see the 80/20 rule applied to business, in my experience the rule applies in relationships, family, fun, and most importantly our search for meaning and purpose.

Very little of our time is spent in valuable space. Essentially four-fifths of our time is outside of the valuable or enriching space. That goes so hard against what we think life ought to be.

In reality there are few things of value. We need to identify what those things are for each of us, focus on those things, grow those things, and make those things better. The 80/20 rule applies uniquely to what we're talking about here. The language of purpose versus the default.

Default is the 80% where we're not satisfied, where there's waste, where there's non-productive or non-rewarding experiences. The 20% is our Ikigai. That's where the language of purpose resides. That's the value that we want to have in our lives.

While we're talking about 80/20 and the language of purpose let's take a moment and take a step back and refresh our memory about our definition of Ikigai.

Ikigai is about expressing our essence and purpose in harmony with whatever we do.

When we talk about Ikigai, what we're really talking about is the 20% in our 80/20 rule. That's where the value is. That's where soundness, wholeness, and completeness are. The 80% is where the disintegration occurs. That's the default language. When we're in our Ikigai, that's our 20% and that's where the magic happens.

This section is focused on giving you a tool to expand, explode, and live into that 20%. It's about growing that 20%. So many people ask me, what if I can't live fully into my Ikigai? Think about the 80/20 rule, 20% of your time right now is the value add. Each moment in your 20% space is 16 times the value. Sixteen times!

With a 16x value you can start seeing a huge difference in your life with even a small addition of time spent. By making that 20% a 21% or 22% you are multiplying those moments of happiness and joy 16 times.

I'm going to give you the tool to expand and explode that 20% and something even more. Remember the essence of our lives is made real by the language that we use.

Now I want you to imagine through the language of purpose, you can describe your 20% to others. Just imagine that. You can use the language of purpose to enlist their support, their help, and their encouragement along the way.

Steven Pressfield wrote in his book, *The War of Art*, "Our job in this lifetime is not to shape ourselves into some ideal we imagine we ought to be, but to find out who we already are and become it."[2]

Breaking that insight down a little further, shaping ourselves into some ideal or who the world tells us we ought to be is the default approach.

Our job, our mission, our one common calling is to uncover who we already are, and then become it. Becoming who you really are is your 20%.

Purpose is on top of the Ikigai Nexus because it is in having an understanding of your purpose that leads to a deeper sense of who you are at your essence and how you can express yourself in harmony with whatever you do.

Let's explore what it means to understand your purpose. The Old English origin of understand meant to comprehend, to read a sign of, and literally stand in the midst of. Coming from the Sanskrit word *antar* or Latin *inter*, it means among or between. Ancient Greek takes the meaning deeper to intestines or gut.

In other words, understanding your purpose means knowing why you are here at your deepest levels and among all parts of your being.

Once you have that sense of purpose, your 20%, you can begin to embody it even if you're surrounded by people using the default language. In modeling yours you open the door for others to discover theirs. When they find their purpose, they can share it with someone else, creating a ripple effect of positive change. Imagine a world where more and more people are operating in their 20%, bringing their unique gifts and talents to the world. Doesn't that sound exciting?

We are each born with a unique combination of things to bring something to the world better than anyone else. The trick is uncovering your combination. Take a moment now to sit with this idea. That your essence and abilities represent a unique combination and bring something to the world no one else can bring.

Ponder that potent insight for a while. Then combine it with living in your 20%. Do that for a few minutes before starting the next section.

Creating Your Statement of Purpose, Your Ikiverse

Since we are each born with the ability to do a unique combination of things better than anyone else, wouldn't it be great to both know what that is and have an easy way to express it?

The nature of our lives is made real by the language we use. Understanding that the language of purpose is about enabling us to express our purpose.

Here's how we're going to use that language to help you identify and live out your purpose. It's your way to quickly enlist support and collaboration around your 20%.

It's called the Ikiverse

Imagine you're at a party and you're networking. We've all been there. What's the first thing people ask you? **What do you do?**

We've all been asked that question, which of course is all about our jobs. Our Ikigai is infinitely richer and more interesting than our current and often temporary occupation.

In defining purpose, many get hung up on wanting a deep and comprehensive philosophical understanding of the one thing they should be doing. They want to know their career or their life partner or some impossible calling like returning the Ring to Mordor in *The Lord of the Rings*. It is so big and so consequential that it is overwhelming, and people freeze. They often end up doing little or nothing.

Begin and Then Become

As with most things, the best way to uncover your purpose is to start small. Even a Kaizen-like terrible version of your "purpose" is a step toward the beginning and when you begin something it becomes. The way we start small is our Ikiverse, our simple and easily understood purpose statement.

This is my original Ikiverse. I've refined it over the years of course, though I'm going to share my earliest version because it exemplifies the small beginning your first Ikiverse will have.

The great thing is you don't have to spend 20 years developing yours like I did. You'll be able to accelerate the process of your Ikiverse and have a first Kaizen "terrible" version even at the end of this chapter.

My original Ikiverse was . . .

I encourage, empower, and enable people to be all they were meant to be.

That's it, straightforward and simple. I've refined it over the years to a much deeper version now. The important thing is this was good enough to get me started and led me to where I am today.

It's also not my job. My Ikiverse is something I can apply to everything in my life. I live out my Ikigai in business, my hobbies, my marriage, and spending time with my grandchildren all from understanding that simple verse.

I've had a unique set of opportunities and experiences to live out my Ikiverse. From being a disc jockey and radio/tv newsman to a Sergeant in the United States Marine Corps to an engineer in two different disciplines. Then later as an IT executive and so forth throughout my career.

Here's the important distinction. I've also been an eighth grade girls basketball coach that led my daughter's team to a sixth place finish in a National Eighth Grade Championship Tournament. I've been a dad, husband, brother, grandpa, runner, and more.

In every one of those things, I'm able to live out my Ikigai. The best moments, and when I'm most alive, are while encouraging, empowering, and enabling people to be all they were meant to be now.

I know there's definitely a few of you who are wondering how this is different from the million other "find your why" exhortations that are out there. Your Ikiverse is deeper than your *why*. Millions of people can have the same "why." Your Ikiverse is unique to you.

Remember when I first said that your mission is to be the most "you" that you can be? Your Ikiverse is unique to you and like you it is one of a kind.

The other difference is your Ikiverse needs to be big enough for a whole lifetime of activities. Not just this part of your life or the next part of your life, it is for your entire lifetime.

Sometimes it is easier to understand when you've been given a bad example. Allow me to give you an example of a bad Ikiverse.

I want to be a good parent and raise happy kids.

We all hope that everybody who has children wants to be a good parent. Also, if you have children, you want your kids to be happy. Obviously, that's not a bad thing.

A good Ikiverse must represent a lifetime of activities. You likely won't be a parent your entire life, at least in terms of day-to-day activity. This only covers your kids and not any other relationships. The other thing that makes this a "bad" Ikiverse is the fact that you can't control other people's feelings. You can't make someone, even your children, be happy.

A better Ikiverse would be . . .

I cultivate an atmosphere of growth, exploration, and infinite possibility in the lives I touch.

That's the Ikiverse of Jane,[3] someone I've coached and who started with the bad verse in the example. The magnificent thing about Jane's Ikiverse is by articulating it in this way she's been able to live it out in every aspect of her life; in her job, marriage, and not surprisingly in being a parent. This Ikiverse informs every aspect of her life.

Think of how much better she can be as a parent when focused on cultivating an atmosphere of growth, discovery through exploration, and the embrace of infinite possibility. Not only now when her kids are little but when they are adults as well. Even when the kids grow up and have kids of their own and her role shifts to being a grandparent. It applies at every stage.

"Cultivating an atmosphere of growth, exploration, and infinite possibility in the lives I touch." Beyond your family, that might include your neighbors or the people you work with or that work for or with you. It could be applied in your church or community. You could even live into it in the five-minute encounter with the barista at your favorite coffee shop. Ikiverse is infinitely more than your temporary "why."

How much more potent is that Ikiverse than the narrow view of what you are passionate about and what someone is willing to pay for?

Think back to the idea of living in your 20% with your 20% being your Ikigai space. Since creating her Ikiverse Jane has found myriad of ways to live it out in her career. She shared her Ikiverse with her employer who then helped fashion opportunities for more time in work that involves creating an atmosphere nurturing growth and infinite possibilities.

In addition to her career, she's been doing some writing about her hobby and as a result developed a large online following. This led her to creating online classes and webinars.

Taking the things she learned about herself in applying her verse at home and job, Jane expanded it to entirely new areas of her life. She is growing her 20%. All this from creating and using her Ikiverse. Remember every minute added to your 20% is worth 16 times the pleasure, enrichment, fun, and reward.

Creating Your Ikiverse

Let's talk about creating your own Ikiverse. Creating your Ikiverse is a deceptively simple process, though it is not a one-time event. What we're going to do here is apply the lessons of Kaizen and do a small thing first.

Your Ikiverse is made up of what I call the Three Vs: **verbs, value,** and **vision.**

Because an Ikiverse is designed to actively help you uncover your Ikigai and enlist the support of those around you, we start with action. That's where the verbs come in. On the next page you will see a list of verbs. Look at the list and circle all that speak to you.

Abundance	Accept	Accomplish	Action	Adventure
Agility	Alignment	Amaze	Appreciate	Audacious
Audacity	Authentic	Awaken	Awesome	Balance
Believe	Bloom	Blossom	Bold	Boundaries
Boundless	Brave	Breathe	Brilliance	Calm
Capable	Celebrate	Change	Choose	Comfort
Commit	Complete	Confidence	Connection	Conquer
Consistency	Contentment	Courage	Create	Cultivate
Dedicated	Deliberate	Determination	Diligence	Discipline
Discover	Efficiency	Efficient	Elevate	Embrace
Emerge	Empower	Encourage	Engaged	Enough
Epic	Epiphany	Essence	Essential	Explore
Faith	Family	Fearless	Fierce	Finish
Flourish	Flow	Focus	Forgiveness	Forward
Freedom	Give	Glow	Grace	Gratitude
Grit	Grounded	Growth	Happiness	Harmony
Healthy	Home	Honor	Hustle	Incomparable
Independence	Inspiration	Inspired	Intentional	Joy
Kindness	Laughter	Leap	Learn	Less
Liberate	Light	Limitless	Listen	Love
Magnetic	Maintain	Margins	Mindful	Minimize
Momentum	Move	Noble	Now	Nurture
Open	Organize	Overcome	Passion	Patience
Peace	Perseverance	Persist	Phenomenal	Pioneer
Plan	Playful	Positivity	Possible	Power
Prepared	Presence	Proactive	Productive	Propel
Prosper	Quest	Radiance	Receive	Recover
Refresh	Relationships	Relax	Release	Relentless
Renew	Resolve	Rest	Revive	Rise
Routines	Self-control	Serendipity	Serenity	Shine
Simplify	Slow	Soar	Space	Spark
Spontaneous	Steady	Strength	Strive	Strong
Structure	Succeed	Surrender	Temperance	Tenacious
Tenacity	Thrive	Today	Transform	Transition
Trust	Truth	Unbound	Uncluttered	Unflappable
Unstoppable	Value	Victory	Vision	Voyage
Welcome	Wellness	Wonder	Worthy	Zest

Printable versions of verb list and other supporting documents are available at davidmarlow.com

No matter how many you circle, eventually you will refine your list down to three. Once you have your verbs let's think about values.

What are your values? Some examples for values are happiness, family, honesty, integrity, faith, peace, kindness, justice, creativity, freedom, excellence. When you think about who you are at your core, what value speaks to you? As with the verbs, you may have many at the beginning; refine your list down to one. Write that one down and it will be used as your core value theme.

The final piece to your Ikiverse is the vision. What or whom do you want to impact? Think about who you are helping and how.

Using the three verbs you selected, one value theme and your vison, begin to create a sentence.

I _____, _____, and _____, (your three verbs)_____, (your core value theme) _____, the impact or people.

In my own example I started with my three verbs . . .

- Encourage
- Empower
- Enable

Earlier I mentioned distinction work, which is an introspective refining of understanding. You'll recall we explored the meaning of an invitation beyond the common definition to an encouragement to go after something, to pursue it with energy and enthusiasm.

In this case we will use this distinction approach to expand our understanding and meaning of the words we've chosen and how they reflect our deeper selves.

There are of course various methods to explore deeper meanings such as meditation, journaling, or discussing with others. Distinction has an advantage over other methods when we're exploring the language of purpose, as it allows us to uncover layers of meaning in words that might not be immediately apparent. In my work I've found this to be a unique benefit of distinction work in our quest for Ikigai. Because it personalizes understanding, it supports creating an Ikiverse that is one of a kind and unique to you.

The nature of our lives is made real by the language we use. The language of purpose is fundamental to this reality. Because we're building from this foundation, distinction work is essential. Let's apply this to the verb "encourage" from my own verse.

When you go to the root word of "encourage" and you dig deeper into synonyms and other meanings, there's a synonym that spoke to me and that is "inspirit." Inspirit means to inspire or "bring to life." For me, encouragement was not about the pat on your back, "way to go," "good job," kind of encouragement. It was about helping people bring to life or create a life with meaning and fulfillment.

This process of distinction work revealed layers of meaning I hadn't initially considered. It transformed "encourage" from a simple concept into something more profound and aligned with my intentions.

Then for my core value theme I selected integrity. Integrity means a great deal more than simply telling the truth or moral principles. The deeper meaning from my distinction work is integrity as in an integrated self, sound, whole and complete. Living with integrity being true to who you are and why you are here.

As with the exploration of my verbs, distinction work allowed me to uncover a more personal understanding of integrity beyond the standard interpretation.

While we apply distinction work to refine our understanding of our verbs and core value, the vision component of our Ikiverse takes a different approach. The vision is about clearly identifying who and how you want to serve. It's a straightforward statement of impact.

My vision was to impact people by supporting them in being who they were meant to be to their fullest potential.

While not requiring distinction work, your vision statement is equally critical to completing our Ikiverse. Once all three components are in place we're ready to create our verse.

As I taught you earlier, using Kaizen practices, start small by writing anything that has come to you. Give yourself permission to create a terrible version. There's no right or wrong way to go about this. This is your Ikiverse. Understand that what you come up with today may or may not be your final version of your Ikiverse. In fact, it probably won't be, because you're going to work with it, use it, and get a deeper understanding of it.

Start small by giving yourself permission to write down anything based on your three verbs, value, and vision. It is super simple and yet it can seem challenging. You may be feeling a little daunted. Understand that this is the beginning, and this is the start for you being able to express your Ikigai to other people and to be able to use it in every aspect of your life. Take one small step of writing anything down, at any level of resolution.

My early Ikiverse was . . .

I encourage, empower, and enable people to be all they were meant to be.

It is easy to see the verbs in this. What might be harder to see is my value, which is integrity. While the word integrity is not literally spelled out, it is represented by the broader meaning in the sentence itself.

If someone is living in an integrated state, they will be able to live out fully all they were meant to be in life. And for my vison, those people who want to live a life of integrity and purpose are the people I want to support.

For a long time, I struggled both understanding and applying my Ikigai because I couldn't express it. I thought it had to have something to do with continuous improvement or efficiency or productivity because that's what I'd been doing an awful lot of. When I was able to take a step back and create my Ikiverse, I could see encouraging, empowering, enabling people to be all they were meant to be could be applied in the large corporate transformation efforts I led.

It could equally be applied to working with individuals and teaching them the personal skills of Kaizen and self-improvement, all of which contributed to the continuous improvement programs. It was easy to see it applied when coaching my daughter's basketball team. Not just basketball skills, but working with them as individuals supporting their growth and development into mature adults as well as learning to play basketball.

All of those things and more. Most recently, being a grandfather might be the best application. My vision is to be fully present and pour love into those kids every chance I get. To be a source of total acceptance and encouragement for them.

In every one of those examples, I encourage, empower, and enable people to be all they were meant to be.

Take a step back to business again where it aligned with my work in developing new products, processes, and services for companies and innovating the companies themselves. In each case, I've found that my greatest successes and satisfaction came when I was able to encourage people to be what they were meant to be.

Beyond encouragement I empower and enable some of the technical and tactical ways for people and businesses to be all they were meant to be. That's done through my coaching and consulting. You can start to see now that having an Ikiverse that I can share with other people facilitates my application of my Ikigai. It also allows others to help me look for new ways to use and live it out.

There is much more to purpose and where you can go with your Ikiverse. This is the beginning and a Kaizen approach. You can and will go deeper as time goes on. Think of this as your running for one minute, walking for four minutes equivalent instead of trying to run a marathon.

Remember my client, Tom? He's the one who had a career coach, life coach, nutrition coach, fitness coach, and an executive coach. None of those people could help him. What ultimately worked for Tom was getting the noise down and then reinvesting that time, energy, and focus in developing his Ikiverse.

Starting with defining his purpose through an Ikiverse enabled him to make immediate changes to his life that led to greater self-awareness, expressing his essence and purpose in harmony with everything that he did.

There's a reason why purpose is on the top of Ikigai image. It's because if we can get that working definition of our purpose we can engage in experiments and tests and can share it with other people, enlisting their support.

By actively trying out our Ikiverse, our purpose statement, we refine our understanding of our purpose. This in turn leads to greater self-awareness. As we understand ourselves better, we create opportunities to act out our essence and purpose in harmony with whatever we are doing. This allows us to express our Ikigai in every aspect of our lives.

Keep in mind Tom was skeptical. Even though he hired me he did not believe this was going to work. I showed him all of the things that I am showing you here in this chapter. I took Tom through a procedure, very similar to what you are doing here.

I'm going to tell you, Tom was a tough cookie. Several of his first iterations were more like mission statements for companies than a personal Ikiverse with results and measurables and things like that in them.

Here's one example . . .

I am dedicated to embracing my innate grit and energy, exceeding performance benchmarks, metrics, and measures, driving transformative personal growth, and shaping my future through meticulous analysis and unwavering dedication.

This is both a terrible version in a Kaizen sense and a terrible version . . . literally. Yours cannot possibly be worse than this. The great thing is by starting with something, it fostered conversation for him. First with me and then with others. Those conversations created an understanding in himself, helping him clarify what he wanted.

Anything you create will likely be better than this and will foster those same kinds of conversations and self-understanding.

In the previous chapters I shared how Tom had "travel" as something he wanted to do more. Looking at his Ikiverse I was able to ask where travel was represented in this. It wasn't, and he reworked his verse to include travel.

Here is the power of the language of purpose. Having even that terrible version helped facilitate the conversation he and I were able to have. Then the revised version supported the conversation with his wife. Tom expressed what he wanted from travel and what he didn't, opening the door for them both to gain greater understanding.

Tom then sat down with his boss. His Ikiverse gave him a clear idea in his own head and an easy way to express where he wanted to be. Tom's boss was open and said, "If you're going to do more of this you can't work more hours. Let's figure out how we could take some of these other things off your plate."

This prompted conversations with his team. Many of the people who worked for Tom as well as some of his peers were looking for growth opportunities in areas Tom no longer wanted to manage. Just like that, the language of purpose had opened up possibilities for many more people to be working on the things they wanted to do.

"What _would you like_ to be doing more of, and how can I help you do it?"

"What do you _need_ to be doing more of, and how can I help you do it?"

Once we start talking in the language of purpose, all kinds of possibilities and opportunities emerge for us and those around us.

I shared Tom's journey in part because he was skeptical, rooted in the language of default and strongly invested in his image as a successful executive. Even so, he was able to create an effective Ikiverse that changed his life. Since you are reading this book, it is unlikely you are as skeptical or rooted in the default as Tom. Your first attempt at defining your purpose won't be worse than his, and his worked wonders. Imagine what yours will do!

The Ikigai Guy's Wife

The story of how my wife, Alicia, came up with her Ikiverse is an example of the process and impact of defined purpose beyond a static "why." She initially struggled, wanting it to be perfect. Not able to come up with anything, I suggested she drop perfection and apply the Kaizen approach of starting small with a terrible version. This gave her freedom to experiment and try, ultimately coming up with this.

Like you, she received the instructions of beginning by selecting as many verbs that were meaningful and circling them. Instead of circles she put dots beside them, which tells you something about my wife and that it doesn't matter how you identify your initial verb list.

Her initial list was dream, touch, produce, sustain, communicate, and implement. You can have as many as you want at the start with the idea to winnow them down to three.

- Dream
- Produce
- Touch
- Sustain

- Communicate
- Implement

Getting it down to three is where distinction work comes in play. We started with dream and what it meant to her. For her, *dream* was an aspiration and connected to doing something in a creative space. *Produce* was particularly interesting to me because it didn't seem to fit until she explained it was about the act of creating. Bringing something about or making it as a creative practice. The more we talked about it, the more we realized that was really the same thing. In the end, "dream" and "produce" were attempts to say "create."

- ~~Dream~~
- ~~Produce~~
- Create
- Touch
- Sustain
- Communicate
- Implement

"Sustain," "communicate," and "implement" were about making her creative work a reality. As we sorted through deeper meanings of all three words, the idea of impacting came into play. Making it happen through a creative act and making it happen in a way that was impactful.

- ~~Dream~~
- ~~Produce~~
- Create
- Touch
- Impact
- ~~Sustain~~
- ~~Communicate~~
- ~~Implement~~

She chose the word *impact* and then went deeper into her selection of "touch." *Touch* for Alicia meant reaching someone at their deepest level through these creative endeavors.

Those became her three verbs, *create, touch,* and *impact.* Now, the interesting thing about that is *create* and *impact* were not words that she selected at any point in time until we did a refinement. It was in that dive into the richer meaning of those words that she identified much more closely with them.

Getting those refined meanings were exciting for her and gave her a better understanding of things she was feeling and wanted in her life. She described it as fun! Which is exactly what the process should be.

For her values, Alicia began with "punctuality," "readiness," "respect," "serenity," and "wisdom." We continued the distinction work we had done with the verbs. Asking, "What does *punctuality* mean to you, what does *readiness* mean to you?"

Researching definitions, synonyms, and root meanings revealed that all five ultimately connected to *wisdom.* Living an effective life, respectful of your time and the time of others. Being ready and capable of doing what you needed to do. All executed so well that it provided a level of serenity. For Alicia these exemplified a successful life.

This theme of a life well lived connected strongly to her views on wisdom and sharing her wisdom with those close to her. Which led to *wisdom* becoming her value theme.

Pulling it altogether, she has actions of "create," "touch," "impact," and the value theme of "wisdom." Alicia was thrilled with the refinement even as she struggled putting them into a sentence.

This is where most people struggle. Even if you aren't a recovering perfectionist like me, that drive to have the right answer is strong. It gets instilled in us from an early age in school and is a destructive part of the default language.

In my coaching and in my own life, I encourage people to give up the need for perfection when you're writing something by employing Kaizen. Start small and release judgment or the need to be perfect.

When writing an article or a post or anything of any value, I'll sometimes sit and stare at a blank page for a while, though not very long. Ultimately, I give myself permission to type a terrible version and remind myself whatever I write is going to be okay.

Next thing I know, I'm typing all kinds of cool stuff. For Alicia, I reminded her of this Kaizen approach saying, "Write something, anything you want."

"You know what I really want to say?" she asked.

"No, I don't. Whatever it is, why don't you say it and make that your verse. What do you really want to say?"

Feeling free to say what was on her mind rather than some image of what her verse had to be released all kind of thought and energy. Alicia wrote down half a page of things that were in her heart though hidden from view.

The first run was more disappointments than her desired purpose. As one example, she wanted to share her wisdom with people, and some close to her weren't willing to listen. It was more centered on disappointments about what wasn't happening than an Ikigai verse.

Still, it was powerful because writing down how she felt opened her thinking. Having something to react to eased talking through those things. In my coaching I often ask if that's the world you want, what would get you there?

For Alicia I asked, "What would it look like if that was happening, if people were listening?" We flipped all the things that weren't happening and created the world she wanted. With that vision she wrote her first version of the Ikiverse.

I impact my people through my wisdom and knowledge. They are touched by what I share, feel joy, love and gain wisdom, through what I create in words, works, or environment.

This is a great start. It captures all that Alicia feels is her calling. It clearly expresses her purpose. The challenge is an Ikiverse needs to be one sentence. She needed something just as meaningful that was shorter and easier to remember and share. We took a moment to celebrate this first version then again applied Kaizen and started making small changes. In the end she came up with . . .

I impact my people through wisdom, and they are touched by what I create.

Alicia sees her purpose as impacting her people through wisdom, and they're touched through that wisdom by what she creates. She talks about her people. Realize you can go for the whole world if you want. For Alicia her people are her husband, children, family, friends, and community. She was a Starbucks barista and included the customers as her people that she would be impacting and connecting with.

This refined verse is simple yet comprehensive, reflecting the fullness of her deeper purpose. It has stood the test of time.

Right after Alicia created this, one of our neighbors lost her mother. Anne's mom was a crocheter, and Alicia crochets. Anne's mother left behind a collection of yarn. It was vintage yarn from the 1970s that was in the colors of the time and more difficult to work with than yarn made today. Because it was her mom's she didn't want to throw it away or give it to just anyone. Anne wanted it to go to someone who would care for it and value it.

She asked Alicia if she would like the yarn. Alicia was touched because of the sentimental value of the yarn and said yes.

She thought immediately of her new Ikiverse . . . "I impact my people through wisdom, and they're touched by what I create." She decided this was an opportunity for her to create something with this yarn for Anne. Alicia made an afghan for Anne from her mother's yarn.

Imagine you're Anne. You gave someone yarn that belonged to your mother. Now they've given you back a handmade piece of art that honors your mother as well as acknowledges the gift you shared. That is Ikigai in action.

That's how my wife created her Ikiverse and then lived it out right away. Since then she's applied it to every area of her life including expanding to add in four grandchildren.

Let's recap what you've learned

The nature of our lives is made real by the language we use. It's important to understand what language you're using, the default language or the language of purpose. When we understand the language and we're using it right we're able to define our Ikigai.

We re-examined the 80/20 rule and learned how it applies to our Ikigai. The 80%, the non-value part of things, is the default language, the default part of life.

We learned the 20%, the valuable part, is our Ikigai. When we're living our Ikigai we're operating in that 20%. By creating and using our Ikiverse we can easily grow that value space. Understanding that for every 1% spent in our Ikigai is 16 times the value of those experiences in the 80%. When we increase time spent in our Ikigai space, even by just 1% (from 20% to 21%), the positive impact on our lives is 16 times greater.

Even a small change, a small movement toward experiencing our Ikigai, adds tremendous value to our lives.

We also learned the power of Ikiverse in terms of creating conversation and opportunities to connect with others. Knowing our Ikiverse energizes us. Then it allows us to talk to others and share it with them, enlisting their support.

It enables us to help others as well. Imagine asking friends or family, "What would you like to be doing more of and how can I help you do that? What do you need to be doing more of and how can I help you do that?" A world were we're all supporting one another and living out our Ikigai.

Your Ikiverse also creates another opportunity which we will explore in the next chapter.

PART

II

The Second Invitation
Uncovering Your Purpose

8

Uncovering Our Essence

IN THE IKIGAI Nexus, purpose is listed on top because the journey begins with understanding our purpose. We focus on getting the noise down in our lives (and careers/businesses) in order to hear that still, small voice of purpose. Then creating a working model of purpose gives us a means to thoughtfully and intentionally explore our essence. It is in this exploration that we uncover more about ourselves.

What I share next are stories and examples of exploration that reveal and express Ikigai. Throughout this chapter, you will read about tactical methods as well as philosophical approaches that are in service to understanding who you are at your deepest levels. At this point, I'll mention I ate an orange for the first time when I was 50 years old.

Pattern-Seeking Creatures

Humans are pattern-seeking creatures. In fact, your brain might already be working overtime trying to find a pattern or connection between my not eating oranges until I was 50 and Ikigai. Don't worry, I'll get to that.

We look for and live in patterns, which can be very good. For example, when you're pulling up to a traffic light. We don't want to have to figure out what red, yellow, and green mean each time we come to an intersection. The downside of pattern thinking is when it locks us into behaviors.

When we're trying to break out of the default space, the default way of life, and start removing those scales off the Thou-Shalt Dragon, we need to break out of the patterns we've been in most of our lives.

Imagine if you took a wooden box, filled it with sand, and smoothed it out to be as perfectly even as possible. Then, if you began dripping water onto it in the same spot, you would eventually create a divot where the water would pool.

After a while, even if you started dropping that water in different spots, it would still flow back to that same original indentation, no matter where above the box you released the new drops.

Our thinking is a lot like that. When you need to change behavior or break out into something new, like getting out of the default mode, it's essential that you're not just dropping water in a different spot above the box.

The way to do that is by trying new things and new ways of doing some of the old things. You've got your Ikiverse, and that's a great start. As powerful as it is to create your Ikiverse, if we do nothing else, we're going to stay in that same sandbox only now with a very cool purpose phrase. There are some easy ways to begin testing and breaking out of your patterns of thinking.

Spilling the Beans on Uncovering and Living Your Ikigai

Like many other things in my life, I came late to an appreciation for coffee, not enjoying it until my mid-30s. Here is the story where I spill the beans on a coffee connection to uncovering and living your Ikigai.

Long Dark Winter

The sun wouldn't rise above the Kettle Moraine for many hours. With the only illumination coming from the dome light, I located the tiny scraper that had been in my car from my time in Texas. It was no match for the thick windshield ice of my new home in Wisconsin. Turning the ignition, the starter whined as if to say, "You're kidding, right?" In the short drive to the office, the car didn't even have time to warm up.

My nose was immediately hit with the aroma of brewing coffee as I entered the building. Even as a kid, I loved the smell of coffee, if not the taste of it.

My parents would drink coffee all day long. My dad would brew it in the morning and let it sit on the burner all day, growing darker and thicker. We used to joke that he could use his end-of-day coffee to patch the asphalt in the driveway. They would buy whatever was cheapest because coffee was coffee.

Months before, my oldest son went on a school field trip to a campground and I was asked to chaperon. Despite not drinking coffee, I did like my morning caffeine, typically a soda. Growing up in Indiana we called everything a coke when referring to a carbonated soft drink. Looking back, it was rather inconvenient. We'd asked for a coke and then had to specify what kind of "coke" we wanted. Mine was typically Dr. Pepper.

Whatever you call it soda, pop, or coke, there wasn't any to be had on this camping trip. We were in the middle of the woods and the only caffeine available was coffee. Facing an inevitable headache from caffeine withdrawal I went for it. There wasn't even sugar or cream available. I told you we were roughing it in the woods.

As expected, it tasted awful. It was bitter and left a bad taste in my mouth, though I noticed I liked the way it made me feel. The second day in the woods coffee and I started a brief relationship.

Back in civilization I quickly returned to my soda routine until that cold, dark morning drive into work. The prior eight years I had spent in warm, sunny places like Hawaii or Texas. This was the first cold and dark winter I had experienced.

Maybe it was the bitter cold, but that morning the coffee smelled particularly enticing. One of the other engineers noticed me eyeing the machine, handed me a mug with the GE logo emblazoned on the side, and invited me to join him. With a 50/50 ratio of sugar and cream to coffee, I held the warm mug and enjoyed a sip. It took the edge off, and like that day in the woods, helped me wake up and feel better.

The relationship remained casual for several years where coffee and I would share a morning only at work and only during winter.

One of the salient aspects of working at GE at the time was it was a global entity. We had recently acquired a medical devices business in France, and I was sent to Paris to start up a GE product team.

The plant was near Versailles in the tiny commune of Buc. An overnight flight to France, train ride from Paris to Buc, and morning full of meetings found me occasionally dozing off despite my best efforts to stay alert. Thankfully my new colleagues were patient as I dealt with my jet lag and offered to break for an early lunch.

The cafeteria wasn't like ours back home. It was luxuriously appointed with chefs preparing fabulous-looking dishes. Golden roasted Cornish hens, hand-tossed pizzas, and more. Everything I had ever heard about the extraordinary food in France was confirmed.

"Veux tu du café?" asked the cashier. Assuming she asked if I was paying for my food from the cafeteria, I pointed to my tray and replied in the best French I could muster. "Oui, yes"

"Non, non," she said, lightly waving her finger back and forth, "Est-ce que tu prends un café?" My new colleague Thierry, behind me in the line, explained that the cashier was asking if I wanted café or coffee after the meal. A mid-afternoon coffee seemed like a blissful remedy.

"Oui, café." I responded. There was no way to know at that moment how much my life would change as a result.

The Magic Elixir

After a lunch of some of the most delicious food I'd ever tasted, Thierry led me to a small smoked-filled area with tiny standing tables. It was my first exposure to an espresso bar. Thierry walked up to the counter, held up two fingers and said to the barista, "Deux expressos, s'il vous plaît."

The barista presented us with two tiny cups, each filled to the brim. I took a sip. Almost immediately, my weariness eased. This wasn't coffee; this pleasant yet slightly bitter liquid was a magic elixir.

For the remainder of my time in France and on every return trip, the answer each day was, "Oui, café." Since that first sip so long ago, I've enjoyed, by my estimate, over 30,000 shots of espresso. Most of those were made and enjoyed at home, prepared by my wife. As luck would have it, a few years after my travels to France and with the kids all in school, Alicia returned to work and became a barista at Starbucks. I now had my own personal barista at home.

The Joy of Little Things

One of the best ways to experience Ikigai is by taking joy in little things. The ritual of enjoying (or making) espresso, a little thing, is a rewarding experience that brings me a sense of satisfaction and pleasure.

Even the cup can be a little thing you enjoy. I have a set of "rocket" shaped espresso cups at home I often use. They are fun and add something extra to the daily routine of drinking coffee. The ones on my trip to France were the more traditional cups and a fun part of the experience as well. The more you incorporate taking joy in little things into your experiments the greater the insights will be.

Professional or Amateur

Because I often share about my love of excellent coffee in my writing and speaking, I've had many people tell me I should open a coffee shop. Here's an important distinction and one you should keep in mind as you move along your Ikigai journey.

I have a passion for drinking high-quality and well-made coffee. Not selling it and not running a store. Something to think about when pondering the connection of your passion to your purpose. Distinguish between passions that are best expressed as interests and passions that become careers.

Here's an easy frame to utilize . . . professional and amateur. The difference between the professional and the amateur is that the amateur only wants to do the fun stuff. Professionals love all of it, or at least the combined experience of all of it. In this definition, I am an amateur coffee lover. Remember my Ikiverse?

I encourage, empower, and enable people to be all they were meant to be.

What excites me would be in helping the shop owner discover their purpose and guiding them in linking it to their business. Showing them how to get the noise down in their process so they could focus on what they love doing. That might be running a business, it might be roasting new blends of coffee, or might simply be connecting with many people every day over a fabulous cup of well-made coffee.

Remember, Ikigai is expressing your essence and purpose in harmony with whatever you do. That is not to say a love of coffee isn't in alignment with my Ikigai. It most certainly can be, and for me, it is. Where and how I express that passion is what makes the difference. Some of your passions and interests are "professional," and some are "amateur," and *either* or *both* can be your Ikigai. My wife is a great example of the "both." Her Ikiverse is . . . **I impact my people through wisdom, and they are touched by what I create.** Serving coffee as a profession fits well into that as does crafting a well-made coffee drink at home for her family.

While working, she was learning new things, growing her skills and connecting with people she cared about at work and at home. Whereas my consumption of great coffee was a way to embrace my passions for learning new things by experiencing them and enjoying them. All expressions of our true selves and our purpose in what we were doing.

Trying new things is essential to uncovering our Ikigai. Which almost brings me back to trying an orange for the first time. To say that I've tried new things through bold experiments in my life would be an understatement.

I walked into a radio station when I was 16 years old and asked for (and got) a job on the air as a disc jockey. I knew so little about the Marine Corps when I enlisted it didn't even occur to me that Marines went to sea. Spoiler alert, they do!

I've left safe and secure jobs to start businesses, ran marathons, swam in shark-infested waters, and a host of other daring tests, experiments, and trials. And when I was 50 years old, I ate my first orange. While eating an orange may not seem as daring as swimming in shark-filled waters, for me it was a big emotional risk to go beyond the default image I had of myself.

I couldn't eat oranges as a kid. Their texture and taste kept me from being able to enjoy not only oranges, but also many other foods that most people seemed to love. The orange experiment when I was 50 came about one day when the cafeteria at work installed a new orange slicer.

It looked like an apple slicer though given the differences in apples and oranges (insert your own joke here) I knew it had to work differently. As an engineer, I was curious to try it and then I wasn't going to waste the orange, so I ate the slices.

They were delicious. Having grown out of my texture aversion, or at least having control of it, enabled me to enjoy oranges for the first time.

Fast-forward a few years to a business trip in Boston and everyone on the team was enjoying raw oysters. I decided if I was ever going to try raw oysters in my life it might as well be in a place where they have great ones like Boston. During that week, I tried them twice at two different restaurants. No, I didn't love them.

What I did love was daring myself to try something new and way out of my comfort zone. Did I mention I didn't eat an orange until I was 50? This has become a whole new area of experimentation and growth for me. I look for things I "couldn't" eat as a kid to try all the time now. There are still some things, even after trying again, that I can't eat. Meatloaf, for example.

Not eating meatloaf is a hill I'm prepared to die on.

Meatloaf aside, my list of can'ts and won'ts is shrinking all the time. My eating identity is in closer alignment with my true self. The oyster breakthrough prompted me to try something else out of my comfort zone on the trip to Boston: getting into a Celtics playoff game at the last minute.

Still in Boston, I was out with the work team and realized the Celtics were in town and had a playoff game against LeBron James and the Cleveland Cavaliers.

Dinner was over and no one else wanted to go to the game so I took an Uber to the arena and waited until just prior to the National Anthem to buy a ticket online at the cheapest possible price. I had a blast.

Finding Versus Uncovering

People ask me to help them "find" their Ikigai, though it is better understood as the process of uncovering. Your Ikigai is already there inside, obscured by the default and thou shalts. Trying, experimenting, and taking some risks reveal things about ourselves that waiting and contemplation can't. It builds confidence in expressing our true selves. Trying different things also supports you in identifying and developing your interests and talents. Finding those "amateur" and "professional" things in your life provides opportunities to figure out ways to express your Ikigai through those talents.

Early on in your Ikigai journey, look for opportunities to uncover and break default patterns, as exemplified in these stories. Try something new, add a bit of fun to ordinary things, or turn a routine moment into something special. Savor experiences more deeply, or dive into understanding how things are made. These small shifts can reveal surprising aspects of yourself, helping you uncover your essence and purpose.

Uncovering our Ikigai may require us to try new things, to break free from the default patterns that keep us boxed in and reveal more of our hidden selves. Other times, the clues have been there all along, hidden in plain sight, in the moments and experiences that have shaped us throughout our lives. In the next chapter, we'll dive into these "achievement stories" and learn what they can teach us about living in alignment with our essence.

These "achievement stories" can come from our childhood passions, our proudest accomplishments, or even our daily experiences of joy and fulfillment. As we'll explore, some of the most powerful clues to our Ikigai can be found in the moments throughout our lives when we felt most alive, most true to ourselves. By reflecting on these moments, we can begin to uncover the essence of who we are and what we're called to do. Some might even involve a tennis ball.

9

The Tennis Ball

REMEMBER THAT ORANGE I mentioned in the last chapter? The one I didn't eat until I was 50? That small moment of daring to try something new was a tiny glimpse into the power of breaking out of our default modes.

Uncovering our Ikigai isn't just about seeking out new experiences. It's also about looking back at the experiences we've already had—the moments when we felt most alive, most like our true selves. I call these our "achievement stories," and they can come from any point in our lives. In the last chapter, we saw how trying new things and breaking out of our default patterns can help us uncover our Ikigai. Now, let's dive deeper into this process by exploring those moments throughout our lives when we felt most aligned with our true selves and purpose.

Playing Catch

Whether you've ever owned a dog or not, you've seen one play catch with a ball. When Alicia and I were first married, like many young couples we got a dog. We adopted the Pet of the Week from the humane shelter in town. He was a bichon frisé and poodle mix. Which is to say an adorable fuzzy mutt who was full of energy. We called him Nimrod after the Biblical hero whose name meant mighty hunter. Nimrod has another meaning: goofball. And our dog was more the latter than anything akin to a mighty hunter.

Nimrod's favorite thing to do was chase a tennis ball. At every opportunity he would bring me a tennis ball, dropping it at my feet for me to throw. I'd throw the ball, and he'd bring it back, repeating this process for as long as I would be willing to throw the increasingly slobbery ball. He never tired of doing it. He wouldn't stop to eat; he lived for chasing that tennis ball.

Achievement Stories

Just as my dog Nimrod found endless joy and fulfillment in chasing his tennis ball, each of us has a unique set of passions and talents that bring us to life. But how do we uncover these clues to our Ikigai, especially if we've lost touch with them over the years?

One impactful place to start is by reflecting on our "achievement stories"—those moments from our past, often from our childhood, when we felt a profound sense of pride, joy, and fulfillment. These are the times when we did something that truly mattered to us, that showcased our natural talents and passions.

For me, some of my earliest achievement stories revolve around creative expression like the essay contest in third grade. As a child, I found immense satisfaction in drawing and storytelling. I could lose myself for hours in a brand-new box of crayons, bringing my imaginings to life on the page.

The Magic Box

There was nothing like it in the whole of childhood. Even Christmas paled in comparison to the completeness of opening a brand-new box of 64 Crayola Crayons.

The smell, the look, the worlds of possibilities contained in that green and orange crayon box with breakthrough "sharpener" innovation.

In Mrs. Davis's first grade class, drawing was a big deal. Even bigger than spelling, and I know because I didn't miss a single spelling word all year. I was the only kid who didn't, and it wasn't my spelling that was celebrated by being posted on the wall above the blackboard before parent–teacher conferences.

It was a tiger, or rather, my drawing of a tiger lying down in a jungle. I'm not sure why tigers fascinated me. Something about the mix of color and the distinction of stripes. It could have been experiencing *The Jungle Book* (the original Disney animation) at the now-historic Indiana Theater. Though I think the tiger was the bad guy in that movie. I was six or seven at the time, I can't recall. Even to this day, tigers are the first animals I want to see when I visit the zoo.

My drawing went on the wall above the blackboard. It was good, and I know it was good because of two things.

When Mrs. Davis showed it to the class, some kids accused me of "tracing" it. Tracing was the ultimate cheat in the kid world of drawing. If the picture was good, the first thing to determine was whether it had been traced. If so, it was immediately discounted as a counterfeit. Fortunately for me, it was easy to prove it wasn't traced, as that assignment had to be completed in class. I'll share the second way I knew it was good in a minute.

My mom came home from the parent–teacher conference with the drawing. Mrs. Davis, my mother would later tell me, said I was an exceptional drawer. Again, nothing about my spelling. Didn't miss a word the whole year, you know. The only kid who didn't.

She gave the drawing to my mom, along with some other examples of my work. There was some additional feedback about David being a fine young man who needs to pay attention more, talk less during class, blah blah blah.

My mom kept almost nothing I made in school. The tiger, she kept. Years later, as an adult, I found it in a drawer, and looking at it without the biased lens of a kid I can say it was a good drawing for a first grader.

It was exceptional for another reason. I finished it. As a kid, I loved coloring. Sky blue, you know, that slightly pale shade of blue visible at the edge of the horizon. I loved that color. It was always the first crayon to be used up.

Everything I would draw, or color, had sky blue in it and lots of it. Everything but the tiger. He was deep in the jungle, and there was no sky to be seen. My love of sky blue took a back seat to the artistic impression I wanted the tiger drawing to have.

I Finished the Tiger

Something I didn't love was finishing a coloring project. Opening a brand-new page in a coloring book, I'd get a vision of what a picture could be and work tirelessly until most of it was colored in. Then, I'd get bored and start another, leaving the first one unfinished.

If my grandmother caught me doing that, she'd make me complete the prior picture before starting a new one. I hated that!

Not the tiger. Unlike the coloring books, there was no drawing to fill in. There was no background to leave undone; the background had to be created. The tiger in the jungle was completely my creation.

That drawing became a symbol of my artistic journey—a reminder that when I poured my whole self into my creative passions, the results could be extraordinary. This full realization, including the fact that I finished the tiger when I never finished pictures, didn't hit me until I started journaling my achievement stories.

My mom kept the tiger, and it was nearly the only thing she ever kept. Thinking about it again almost makes me want to go out and buy a new box of 64 Crayola's right now. We did without a lot growing up. Yet, I always had a new box of crayons to start the year. David, you know, is an exceptional drawer.

There's a Lesson Here

The tiger and the governor's writing contest were achievement stories that revealed an inner creative drive. A passion for storytelling in many mediums. Through art, the written word, and performance. They were rare bright spots as I faced frequent discouragement and obstacles in pursuing my dreams. After winning the writing contest I wanted to write more.

Looking back, I can see key points in my life where my love of storytelling was discouraged or even openly mocked by people close to me.

My parents didn't read my stories. Even my beloved maternal grandmother, the one who wanted me to finish a page in the coloring book. She was loving and encouraging in everything but big dreams. And to my dismay she wouldn't read my stories.

Mr. Joseph[1] was one of my junior high teachers, who also coached a sport. After practice one day I caught a ride home with him because it was raining. In our conversation I shared my dream to be a published author. He proceeded to tell me how difficult that was and that I would never be a writer. I insisted that was what I wanted to do, and he continued by telling me that was foolish, saying again that I would never be a writer and should set a more realistic goal.

At practice the next day some of the other kids on the team started making fun of me about my writing. Apparently, Mr. Joseph shared my "ridiculous" idea about becoming a writer with them, openly mocking me to my teammates. I left practice that day and never went back. I told my parents I hadn't made the team rather than share the real reason.

Writing for school wasn't supportive either. Instead of a source of encouragement for creative expression, writing became a task reduced to rules and formulas, requirements and constraints, of right and wrong.

Looking back, I can see that these experiences hinted at some of my deepest passions and talents—a love of creative expression, a desire to bring joy and beauty into the world, a longing to be seen and appreciated for my unique voice.

Of course, at the time, I wasn't aware of the significance of these experiences. I was just a kid doing something I loved. But that's the power of achievement stories. They hold clues to our Ikigai, even if we don't recognize them as such in the moment.

To get the answers we need in life, we must ask the right questions. If you can ask yourself questions, you can uncover your Ikigai, even if you have no idea what you are called to do today. One of the best questions for uncovering your Ikigai is the one inspired by my dog Nimrod: What's your tennis ball?

For me, my tennis ball—the thing I could do all day, the thing I could do and forget to eat—is to tell a story. Whether writing, speaking, illustrating, or recording a story, it is something I could do all day and then some. Not just any story, of course. The stories that are my tennis ball are stories of encouragement, teaching, or giving the tools for someone to live out their best life.

Notice anything about that? It closely aligns with my Ikiverse to **encourage, empower, and enable people to be all they were meant to be.**

As I shared in previous chapters, there were glimpses of Ikigai early on in my life. I'd love to say the message in these events was obvious to me all along as I started my Ikigai journey. Like many such insights, over the years the once easily visible part of my purpose was hidden by the default world, by disappointments, and even well-meaning family and friends. The example of my coach being only one.

My tennis ball is evident to me now. If yours isn't, spend some time in reflection on your achievement stories. Times in your life, especially your young life when you did something you were especially proud of or something that was fulfilling.

It was in reflecting on the tiger from first grade and the third grade writing contest that I realized things about myself that had been hidden for decades. In those stories are glimpses of my Ikigai. Not just the successes either. Even the discouraging experiences served as an indicator and became part of uncovering as well.

Is writing or storytelling my Ikigai? No, they are ways I express my Ikigai. They aren't even my tennis ball. My tennis ball is creating, which is an important distinction to make as we go forward. Creating is more directly connected to my essence, who I am at my deepest levels.

Digging Deeper

To uncover more of your Ikigai, use insights from your tennis ball reflection to explore the concealed clues in your achievement stories more deeply.

Stories can range from obvious achievements, like my childhood tiger drawing or the writing contest win, to more subtle indicators, such as the pride I felt in getting all the spelling words right. Or the adult accomplishments in transforming teams and businesses I shared in previous chapters. Things that matter to me, things that drove me that made me experience joy and more of myself.

In revisiting these achievement stories, you can uncover buried parts of yourself. Achievement stories reveal aspects of ourselves that might otherwise remain hidden, offering valuable clues to our Ikigai.

In my own experience, I had forgotten how much it meant to win that writing contest and inspire those around me in the second reading group. It wasn't just winning something. I didn't even know there was a contest. It was something I cared about and was good at, something I did that was recognized which made an impact.

In looking back on that achievement story, I also had forgotten all the times people had discouraged me from my writing, much like the example with my coach. Not only did he tell me I couldn't be a writer, he also betrayed my trust and belittled my aspiration to the other kids. His was the most egregious though not the only one.

Let me take a moment to just say that I don't blame or have any bitterness toward him or anyone. Many times, people are expressing things out of their own hurts and failures, or they're trying to save you from pain that maybe they've experienced themselves. Dreaming of being a writer, especially as a young person, is a big stretch.

As you're reflecting, I recommend you embrace the feelings that you experienced at the time, so you understand how they impacted your image of yourself. At the same time, understand that this uncovering process is about getting you to live out your Ikigai in its fullness. Living out the life you were created to live. It's not about blame. It's not even about identifying the cause. At its deepest level, it's about uncovering all that stuff that's been heaped on our true nature and getting rid of it so we can live out the life we were created to live.

What's your tennis ball? What is it that you just love doing so much that you would do it over and over and over again all day long if you could? What have you ever done in your life that's made you forget eating? For me, I can sit down and write or tell a story or create some images or edit some video and put all of that together and then realize it's eight o'clock at night. What have you done in your life that's similar? And maybe it's something you haven't done for a long time or something that you used to do that you don't do anymore.

It could be a series of things that you enjoy doing. Like for me, I love learning. Over the years at Christmas, my kids have gotten me some interesting gifts, like a mushroom-growing kit. I grew edible oyster mushrooms to go on pizzas. Because it was such a unique gift and learning opportunity, I found it captivating. Another year they gave me a beer brewing kit.

Learning the process of brewing and tasting beer at its freshest can be an engrossing exploration. Here's a thing to note: it didn't prompt me to start my own brewery or even take up home brewing as a hobby. What got me excited and what kept me interested was learning something new and learning about the process of how things worked.

The mushrooms and the beer were standalone events, but the theme embedded in both was learning something new. Look for themes in your life when you're thinking about what your tennis ball is. Those themes are clues to uncovering your Ikigai.

After you've spent some time with the tennis ball question and are ready to go deeper, consider how you might get life to "throw the ball" for you more often. Look for ways to create more tennis ball moments.

Also consider what activities or moments make you lose track of time. What do you do that makes you forget to eat? For me, it's things like diving into a new subject, mastering a new skill, or writing.

Good Days and Bad Days

While engaging in our "tennis ball" reflection is crucial, it's equally important to scrutinize our day-to-day experiences. These everyday moments, both positive and negative, can provide invaluable insights into our Ikigai. One effective way to uncover these insights is through a technique I use in my design work called empathy interviewing. This approach can be equally powerful when applied to your self-reflection.

Empathy interviewing is an intensive listening exercise where you invest in understanding someone at their core. One of my favorite starter questions, especially for people not accustomed to reflection, and one that will work for you in your Ikigai reflection, is to ask someone about their most recent good day.

Don't ask them about their favorite day or what would be their perfect day because people will fill in those blanks with what they think they ought to say, what they should say, what they're supposed to say.

Asking someone or asking yourself for details from the most recent good day will drop barriers and allow your thinking to reveal what actually was going on that day. All of this is an effort to prompt reflections on those moments where we are most alive. Reflect on that question for yourself. When was your most recent good day?

- Where were you?
- Who were you with or around?

- What were you doing?
- Why was it a good day?
- Were there moments or things that were especially good about that day?

Then you can ponder when was your last bad day. Ask yourself those same follow-up questions.

- Where were you?
- Who were you with or around?
- What were you doing?
- Why was it a bad day?
- Were there moments that were especially bad during that day?

The Good, the Bad, and the Ugly

I employed this technique with a team struggling to work through significant organizational changes. Going into the project, the leaders told me, and I believe they meant it, they wanted everybody to enjoy their jobs. There were strong indications no one was enjoying their jobs, including increasing absenteeism and a high rate of turnover in a company with industry low turnover in other departments.

I sat down with one member of the team who we'll call Sarah.[2] She was reluctant at first to talk about her experience as part of this team. We sat for a while and talked about the weather, her hobbies, everything except work.

When Sarah relaxed enough to feel comfortable talking about her job, she told me her team was a fabulous group of people. They were all working hard together to do the right things for the company and the customers. She wondered why a project such as mine was even necessary "because everything was great."

After a few minutes of allowing her to share whatever was on her mind, I asked her to "Tell me about a good day, better yet, tell me about your most recent good day at work. When was that?" Her answer startled me.

She began sharing about a "marvelous day" where lots of good things went on, none of which appeared to have anything to do with work. Here's the kicker. Her last good day was three months prior.

We explored her good day for a while with the questions I shared previously, diving into why this particular day was a "good day."

Then I asked her about her most recent bad day. In two seconds, she said, "Yesterday!" Sarah's most recent good day, one which didn't seem to actually have anything to do with work, was months ago and hard to recall, and her last bad day was right at the tip of her tongue.

The value in asking these kinds of questions comes from breaking down the walls of default we all put up when answering. Sarah wanted to believe her job was great. She had convinced herself that she and the team were working hard (which they were) and doing great work, which unfortunately they weren't. The good day/bad day frame helped extract insights into how hard the job had become. Every one of these people wanted to do a good job. The team members wanted to do right by the company and the customer. What the conversation with Sarah and others confirmed was the job had become nearly impossible to do successfully.

Ask yourself these same questions. When you honestly and objectively evaluate your recent good and bad days, you sidestep the human tendency to say what you think you should or what is the "right" thing to say.

The leaders of this team were asking their people how things were going, and the team was telling them what Sarah initially told me. All the while the vast majority were suffering from burnout and exhaustion.

By stripping away the layers we were able to identify the barriers preventing the team from having far more good days than bad. These questions can provide the same support for you.

Let's review . . .

- **What's your tennis ball?**
  o Look for themes and trends.
- **How do we get someone else or life in general to throw the ball for us?**
  o How might I invite more opportunities to chase the tennis ball?
- **What do I do that makes me forget to eat?**
  o When was the last time I was so focused on something I forgot to eat?

- **When was the last good (or bad) day you had?**
  - Where were you?
  - Who were you with or around?
  - What were you doing?
  - Why was it a good (bad) day?
  - Were there moments that were especially good (bad) during that day?
    - How might I bring more of the "good" day elements into my life?
    - How might I eliminate the bad day elements?
- **What are some of your earliest "achievement stories"?**
  - What did you love to do as a child that brought you joy and a sense of accomplishment?
  - How did these experiences make you feel about yourself and your unique talents?
- **Have you ever been discouraged from pursuing a dream or passion, like I was by my gym teacher?**
  - How did this experience affect you at the time?
  - Looking back, what insights can you gain from this experience about your true calling and the opinions of others?

Tennis Lessons

Clues to our Ikigai are scattered among our memories and dreams. By paying attention to those moments when we felt most alive, we uncover signs of our talents and passions.

By reflecting on these early inclinations of our "tennis ball," we uncover precious parts of ourselves hidden by time, discouragement and the default.

Spending time even now pondering our good days and bad days can reveal moments when we are experiencing our Ikigai by expressing our purpose and essence.

And finally, those roadblocks, barriers, and painful times of discouragement can be wayfinders to uncovering our hidden self. By flipping them we generate new dreams and aspirations. Much like the book you are reading now was for me.

10

All Models Are Wrong

WE'VE ALL SEEN the model of what an atom looks like. They call it the planetary model because it looks like a solar system. Its use dates back over a century.

Apparently, it is wrong. I don't mean kind of wrong. It is completely and totally wrong. Yet even though it is incorrect, it makes sense to use it as the model because it advances our ability to understand concepts of the universe.

"All models are wrong, but some are useful." George E. P. Box[1]

I like what Box said because knowing all models are wrong, although some are useful, frees us to operate with our current understanding and make our best guesses based on it. Much like with Uzumaki, we never finish growing in our knowledge. Instead, rather than waiting for perfect information we operate with our best concept and take action today. A good understanding is one that holds together long enough to get you to a better concept.

Another way to think of it is "the map is not the territory." Just as a map is not the actual territory, our perception is not reality. We don't want to confuse our impressions of reality with reality itself.

At various points in our lives we will think we have the answer. It's always best, however, to remember all models are wrong, and some of them are useful. Including the Ikigai Venn Garden that we talked earlier in the book.

Think of your current understanding of your purpose, your first draft of your Ikiverse as a model of learning. It doesn't have to be perfect; in fact, it can't be if all models are wrong. It only must hold together enough to help us live toward a better understanding.

Shakers and Perfection

Even if you aren't a recovering perfectionist like me, the need for things to be "just right" is why most of us aren't fully engaged with living out our Ikigai. We've touched on the idea of the 80/20 rule and will again in greater detail later. In connection to our perfectionist tendencies, it is enough to know that few things matter in life. Very little of what we do brings us most of our positive results. Focusing on those few things that have positive results is better than trying to make everything perfect.

If you are struggling with making everything perfect or waiting to act until everything is ideal, remind yourself of the 80/20 principle in depth. It will make a difference for you. There are few things of value; focus on those things, grow those things, and make those things better.

The Shakers were a small Christian religious movement dedicated to among other things simple living. While their religious practice has faded, many of their principles remain and are manifest in elegant though simple Shaker furniture design.

Created with a minimalist and sustainable focus, there is a raw beauty in the pieces, which follows the Shaker philosophy.

Don't make something unless it is both necessary and useful; but if it is both necessary and useful, don't hesitate to make it beautiful.

The Shakers understood few things mattered and focused on those things while adding in high-value elements of beauty along the way.

Thomas Merton, a Catholic Trappist monk, said of the Shakers, "The peculiar grace of a Shaker chair is due to the fact that it was built by someone capable of believing that an angel might come and sit on it."[2]

John Wilson was a celebrated woodworker who followed the Shaker traditions, specializing in the creation of Shaker boxes.

He embraced the Shaker philosophy, saying, "They had a definition of perfection as being the best you can do today. So, the perfection is progressive. What you can do tomorrow might well need to be a little better."[3]

That is the kind of perfection we seek. Though I'm not sure any Shakers were aware of Kaizen, this idea of perfection is, pardon the pun, perfectly aligned. Small incremental learning, progression, and change mixed with a level of acceptance and joy in the present.

Our Ikigai journey is like that. Let's play with this Shaker idea a bit and make it about Ikigai. A description of Ikigai as being the best you can comprehend today. Our understanding is progressive. How much you can understand and can express tomorrow might well need to be a little deeper.

We can apply this to our understanding as well as our practice of Ikigai. It is the best we can do today while making small increments toward amplified understanding and expression.

- How might the idea that "all models are wrong, but some are useful" be helpful in understanding your Ikigai? Can imperfect models still help you gain insight?
- What parallels do you see between the Shaker philosophy of making things necessary, useful, and beautiful, and the concept of Ikigai? How could you apply this approach to your own life?
- In what ways has striving for perfection held you back from fully engaging with your Ikigai? How can focusing on the most important 20% help you make progress?
- How can adopting the idea of "perfection is progressive" guide you as you deepen your understanding and expression of your Ikigai over time?
- How can being aware that your perceptions may not match reality help you on your Ikigai journey as your understanding evolves?

Way Open

"What if I miss my calling?"—I wondered about this frequently as a teenager, convinced that God had one explicit path for me and that if I didn't somehow find it, I would not live out my purpose. Mixed in with equal measure was a fear that even if I found my calling it would be something I wouldn't enjoy. No wonder I was anxious most of the time.

Courses of study, girlfriends, jobs, whatever. Each time a path would end I'd feel like I had wasted time going down the wrong track when the right one was still out there for me to find.

My first career was in radio and television as an announcer and newsman. When it became apparent that wasn't my ultimate path, I felt like I had wasted those seven years of my life. The same thing when I left the military. It seemed all I had were closed doors.

Quakers are another Christian denomination that, unlike the Shakers, is still active today with close to 400,000 practicing members worldwide. Although it is not my tradition, many members of my family follow Quaker faith practices.

There is an old Quaker saying, "as way opens." Meaning we should proceed as if a way will be revealed. Until then wait patiently for the way to be revealed.

In my own life I kept waiting, though impatiently, and trying things to see if it was "way open" or not. Mostly what I experienced was "way closed."

I can relate to the author Parker J. Palmer who wrote in his book *Let Your Life Speak*[4] that he had reached middle age and still no way open had appeared. It wasn't until an older mentor shared that in their long life, they had never experienced an open way but had many times witnessed a way closed that provided guidance.

In my own experience, closed doors or ways have guided more often than any singular open door or opportunity.

A way closed can be just as useful as way open for guiding us on our Ikigai journey. If you think about it, a door closing tells us that is not our path while leaving open an infinite number of other possible paths. We can celebrate the fact there are many ways still available to us to express our Ikigai.

On top of guiding us, a path that eventually closes can serve as preparation for the time when a way does open. My writing and speaking skills were developed in the highly competitive world of broadcasting when I was only a teenager. Even though that career ended, those skills remained with me throughout my life and have served me in nearly everything I have done since, personally, and professionally. Not to mention, I met my wife because of my broadcasting career.

The Blind Date

Alicia's dad had retired and decided to move from Washington State back home to Indiana after she finished high school. She decided to accompany them and attend college in Indiana.

A year later, while working in a retail store, she and a co-worker were listening to me on the radio while they folded clothes. Her co-worker, Chris, was a friend of mine whose sister I had dated. (It was a disaster, so don't ask.) After the breakup, Chris and I had remained friends. She occasionally called me on the "hotline" to request a song.

That day at the store, Chris wondered if Alicia would like to go out with a group of friends to see a movie. "I'm inviting the guy on the radio," who of course was me.

Alicia said sure, and Chris called the hotline to invite me. Neither of us was interested in meeting anyone or starting a relationship, so going out with a group sounded like low-commitment. The "group" ended up being only four of us, Chris, her boyfriend, Alicia, and me. Our mutual friend had set us up on a blind date.

Alicia and I went out the next weekend, and every weekend after, marrying the following year. We have been together ever since, living in six states and 11 homes—spanning four decades.

Our blind date almost didn't happen. Months before, I was working at a different radio station. The owner had bought the station so that his son could be on the radio because he frankly wasn't good enough to make it on his own.

The son followed me on the air, his show starting right after mine ended. He was notorious for being late. For weeks, I'd finish my show, intro the last song, and sign off. Then I'd set up the next record for him and get ready to go home, only for him to be running late.

It was getting to be both an irritation and a professional embarrassment because it disrupted the finish of my show and the beginning of his. One day he was half an hour late, and having had enough I confronted him.

"At least give me a call and let me know you are going to be late." I wasn't even protesting him being late, asking only for the courtesy of being told ahead of time. While his dad owned the station, the son technically was the general manager, and he promptly told me that if I didn't like it, there was the door.

I responded, that wasn't necessary. All I needed was a heads up so that I could finish my show, doing my sign-off like I wanted. He again said, this time shouting, "If you don't like it, there's the door" and pointed to the door.

We went back and forth several times with each declaration that "there's the door" getting louder. Finally, as the record was about to end, I said, "Okay," pushed back from the microphone, got up out of the chair, walked over to the wall, took down my radio operator's license and quit.

As luck would have it, another radio station in town had been looking for a way to steal me away. Because my ratings were the highest in the market, they wanted to hire me away and eventually put me on another station they owned in a much larger market.

The next day when I called them to talk about a job, there was one already waiting for me. As part of the offer, they dangled an eventual promotion to their big market station in another state. I took the job, though for a whole host of reasons I eventually turned down the promotion.

As it happens, about that time the mid-day announcer, let's call him Marv,[5] decided to quit. He was in a local band. They had become popular in the region and decided to go on a road tour. I was given his show, which, by coincidence, aired during the time slot my future wife listened to while at work.

There is no way I could have planned any of that. Nor could I have anticipated what happened a year later: Marv's band folded, and I was let go so he could have his old job back. It was almost as if the entire reason I was at that station was to meet my wife and not one bit of it was through my careful planning or any insight I had into my calling.

As a friend once encouraged me, "Don't be ashamed of your story. God rarely leads in a straight line." Life may have had some twists and turns along the way. It may not have gone or been going the way you thought it should or hoped it would. All you've done or been through up to this point has played a part in your Ikigai story.

I look at my career and think of being in radio/TV, a United States Marine, an engineer, or an executive. All ended in some way and yet none were failures or the wrong thing. Each of these experiences offered new insights, learnings, and helped shape, in part, who I have become. Turns out I never did have an "ultimate" career, and looking back I couldn't be happier about that.

All too often, our inner critic, voicing the language of default, weighs in to judge. It's a bit like what Jean Cocteau was talking about when he said, "The course of a river is almost always disapproved of by its source."[6]

What if, instead of judging, you embrace the story of the crooked path? What if it's okay that life has turned out differently than you planned? How might embracing your story in this way change the next chapter? How might that lead you to your Ikigai?

- Have you ever worried that you might "miss your calling" or not find your true purpose? How can the idea that "God rarely leads in a straight line" help reframe that fear?
- How have you experienced "closed doors" in your life, and how can you view those as guidance rather than failures?
- Can you think of any skills or relationships that developed through your "closed door" experiences and ended up serving you later on? How can you appreciate those unexpected benefits?
- Do you relate to my experience of feeling like I "wasted time" on paths that didn't end up being my ultimate career? How can adopting a more open mindset about your story help?
- Think about embracing the "crooked path" of life rather than judging it. How might that shift in perspective influence how you approach the next portion of your Ikigai journey?

You may be thinking, "Dave, so far, you've told me all models are wrong and life doesn't go as planned. Great, now what?" I did that with intention, which coincidently is what the next chapter is about.

11

The Path of Intention

THROUGHOUT MY LIFE there have been many more closed doors than open. That continues of course; the difference now for me is Ikigai. The "what" isn't as important as who I am and why I am here.

Being able to articulate that with my "model" of an Ikiverse helps me navigate those openings and closings and get value out of each.

Coddiwompler

We've considered an Ikigai connection to Shakers and Quakers, now let's explore Coddiwomplers. To coddiwomple is to travel purposefully (or intentionally) toward an unknown destination. It is a journey taken simply for the pleasure of the journey itself. This spirit of openness, curiosity, and purpose aligns perfectly with the Ikigai journey.

You have your working model of your Ikigai through your Ikiverse, which gives you the "why." As you begin working on understanding yourself, the "who" emerges. With a "who" and "why," the "what" becomes less important. Taking the approach of a coddiwompler allows you to explore and test myriad ways you can express or experience your Ikigai.

If I had been able to take a step back and look at my early careers through the lens of a coddiwompler with an understanding of my Ikiverse, I'd have seen them differently. Instead of viewing them as missteps or dead ends, I would have recognized these experiences for what they ultimately were: opportunities to learn more about myself.

They were explorations in ways that I could express my Ikigai in terms of a career. I wouldn't have seen them as failures because they weren't. I can, in retrospect, recognize that those careers provided vital things for my learning, growth, and development along the way that equipped me to do what I do today.

Without those experiences it is unlikely I would have been ready to take advantage of the other career opportunities that I had later. I also would not have learned vital insights about myself, leadership, professionalism, and more that served me in all the other roles I had in my life, both in business and in my personal life.

Being a Coddiwompler

What would it mean to travel, as a coddiwompler, purposefully or intentionally toward an unknown destination? With intentionality comes focus, with that focus comes opportunities to see those open and closed doors, as well as chances for you to learn about yourself and what things best embody your Ikigai.

Take running, for example. Running isn't a career, at least not for me. After my shoulder surgery, I looked for ways to stay fit and healthy. In exploring running, I found a perfect alignment, in part because my Ikiverse is to encourage, empower, and enable others to be all they were meant to be.

Running as a sport can be competitive, though it doesn't have to be. To express this part of my Ikigai, I didn't want to be competitive. I wanted to be able to test myself, to grow and explore. I was able to apply my improvement practices, while encouraging others to do things that will support them in being fit and healthy. The way I approach running provides a perfect template of encouragement, even if people aren't interested specifically in running.

My running has encouraged family, friends, and clients to take up exercise. They don't always take up running. Often, it is walking because walking has the similar benefits without some of the downsides that other people experience. I happen to like those downsides, but they don't.

Having a working model of my Ikiverse and embracing my inner coddiwompler, I traveled to an unknown destination. I had no idea where running would take me, literally or figuratively. Even though the ultimate outcome remained a mystery when I started running, there was intentionality in beginning.

I was exploring running to uncover things about myself, to connect with my daughter who was a runner, for fitness, and for a whole host of reasons. Exploring with intentionality and using Kaizen, I knew I could uncover more about myself and grow in a way that supported me emotionally.

As I have shared before, my love of running, coffee, and my grandchildren are all examples and models that I use to illustrate the ways of Ikigai. While not advocating you become a runner, I do want you to embrace your inner coddiwompler.

- What prompts curiosity and exploration for you?
- How might you create more opportunities to explore those things?
- How might life be more vibrant if you do not always have a fixed destination?
- What beliefs might be holding you back from embracing your inner coddiwompler?
- What is one small thing you could do today to embrace the sense of play and spontaneity of a coddiwompler in your daily life?

Apply the Learning

Building on your Ikiverse, your working model of purpose, we've added an understanding of Ikigai perfection in the Shaker definition— perfection as being the best you can do today. We have a working model from the Quakers of an approach to open and closed doors in life. Finally, we have the purposeful or intentional wandering approach of the coddiwompler.

Now it's time to move from theory into practice by applying these principles and approaches to uncovering your Ikigai. Doing the things you've long talked about, but never quite gotten around to, is an excellent place to begin.

Doing the Things

My embrace of coddiwomple started in earnest nearly two decades ago. I had some changes and events in my life, including losing a friend to suicide, which prompted me to start doing the things I used to talk about doing but never did. I didn't realize it then, but starting to do those things was an Ikigai approach to life, and an embrace of wandering intentionally if ever there was one.

One of those things involved ice fishing. My good friend Aaron loves ice fishing. I remember asking him, "So you go out on lakes and cut holes in the ice you are standing on . . . you mean like on purpose?"

Never having been, I thought it was time I tried a quintessential Wisconsin experience. We had talked about going for several years and never actually scheduled the time.

After my friend's death, I declared, "This is the year I'm going to start *doing the things*, and ice fishing is the first. Let's pick a date." Because the lakes don't always freeze early in winter, we picked a date in January when we knew the ice would certainly be ready.

January was especially cold that year. A few days ahead of our scheduled date the weather turned bitter. Single digits with extreme wind. Aaron asked if I wanted to reschedule. "Nope. We are doing it." We went ice fishing in some of the coldest temperatures I had ever experienced, and it was a blast. One of the best times I've ever had, mostly because I followed through. Since then, I've done a number of those things I'd said I wanted to do but never did, and every time I say, I/we should do X, it gets planned.

Taking Action

My wife and I were watching *Blown Away* a while back. It's a group of artists competing in glass-blowing, similar to the cooking contest shows. I commented that I had always thought that would be a cool thing to learn.

"Yes, you have said that many times over the years," she said. That's when it hit me; this is "one of the things!" A quick online search followed and there are indeed local glass-blowing classes available. This was a powerful Ikigai insight and one I continue to follow. As with the beer and mushrooms experiments in previous chapters, I'm probably not going to start making art with glass. In fact, I almost certainly won't, though that does sound cool, doesn't it?

There is something in this for me to uncover about myself and my Ikigai. Following through, doing what I talk about has greatly enhanced my life and given me some of my best experiences. It has also helped me uncover aspects of my Ikigai I would never have realized otherwise. Maybe this is the year you start doing the things you've always talked about doing.

Exploring Interests

Another way to apply the learning is in exploring interests. My father had an impressive curiosity. We'd be on a drive, and he'd stop to "see what there is to see," at a historical marker or place that looked interesting. When my kids were little, we'd be near something interesting and one of them would ask about it. I'd follow my dad's lead and respond, "We have time, let's go over there and take a look."

Someone who took a similar approach to life was Ruth Asawa, a renowned American sculptor whose life provides us with a magnificent example for uncovering our Ikigai. While enduring the injustice of racial prejudice, she remained open to possibility, embracing serendipity, leading to opportunities that guided and developed her art.

Her first foray into art was learning to draw as a child in an internment camp for Japanese Americans during World War II. While in the camps, she was taught drawing by three fellow internees who happened to be Disney artists.

Once released from the camps, Ruth was not allowed to go to college on the West Coast and instead enrolled at Black Mountain College in North Carolina. As luck would have it, she arrived at Black Mountain in 1946, when modernist icon Josef Albers was overseeing the art program there.

Asawa came into her own as an artist while studying under Albers and renowned artists John Cage and Franz Kline. Something I found fascinating, she was also mentored by Buckminster Fuller, who was not an artist at all but more an engineer and innovator.

In researching her life, I watched her mostly self-narrated documentary *Ruth Asawa: Of Forms and Growth*.[1] Throughout, she explains her work as, "something that interests me . . . or, I'm interested in the movement of . . . or, I find it interesting to explore."

Her entire expression of art was understanding, exploring, or testing what interested her. Early on, she explored drawing and became fascinated with creating lines. Then she became interested in turning the lines from drawing into three-dimensional objects, which led her to create elaborate folded paper sculptures.

With the encouragement of Fuller, she would later explore another area of interest, creating structure by extending the lines into metal frames. Fuller, being an architect and designer, added another dimension and perspective to her art.

Her skills and mediums continued to grow and change as she followed what interested her. She explored an entirely new art form by making face masks of unglazed ceramic in the likeness of family, friends, and fellow artists such as photographer John Gutmann.

Over a period of 45 years, Ruth made 233 masks in all. In her later years, her interests led her to make public art, and promote art in and to her community. She made fanciful and often controversial public fountains. The fountains represented a complete departure from anything she had made before. Even so, she became known as "the fountain lady" in her hometown of San Francisco.

Two things about Ruth's life struck me: how curious she remained throughout her life and the complete lack of bitterness despite enduring many more hardships than I've room to share here.

"I hold no hostilities for what happened; I blame no one," she said. "Sometimes good comes through adversity. I would not be who I am today had it not been for the internment, and I like who I am."

Ruth Asawa uncovered her Ikigai through following what interested her and remaining open to possibilities even during the most challenging times.

There are so many lessons in Ruth Asawa's story and my ice fishing story. Let's take a moment to look at them. In my story, I can't tell you how many times over my life I've said that someday I ought to do something and then never did it.

Since that day on the aptly named Wind Lake in Wisconsin, I've been doing "those things." As a result, opportunities for connection and fun have opened for me. My friend Aaron and I, already with a close relationship, left the ice that day with a richer, more nuanced relationship. For one thing, I had shown a genuine interest in something he was passionate about. It gave him a chance to share his knowledge and skills with a close friend. We all love being able to show others something we do well.

Since that time, I see myself in a new light as someone who is open to trying and experimenting with new things, even silly things. A few months ago, I was in my hometown having dinner with my family, who still live there. One of the waitresses had unique earrings. They were Hot Wheels cars, like you would buy at the store, but they were small enough to be earrings.

I was a kid when Hot Wheels were introduced and wondered who took the time to make Hot Wheels cars into little earrings.

I asked her if they were real cars. She said, "Yes, they're real cars. Aren't they cool?" We talked with her for a few minutes and as she left, she remarked I'd made her day. Of course, she made my day as well because it was interesting to me.

By asking about the earrings, I was following an interest. The more you do that, the more you add richness to your life, the more you provide opportunities to connect with people, and the more you find those things that you might be interested in.

In Ruth Asawa's case her interests led her to her life's calling. Keep in mind, her Ikigai wasn't to be a particular type of artist. She changed mediums routinely. If we think in terms of her tennis ball, it was to follow her interests, and her purpose was to connect to people with a message of hope, forgiveness, and beauty.

She expressed who she was at the deepest levels through following her interests and lived those out in harmony with whatever she did. That is Ikigai.

I'm finding ways to act on my interests and embrace the present by "doing the things" and not waiting.

In exploring and pursuing interests I encourage you to embrace moments of serendipity. Serendipity means experiencing good luck or fortune while making unexpected and fortunate discoveries. One such event occurred for me in 2016.

I'm a recovering perfectionist. For way too long in my life, I was uptight and anxious. I've learned over the years that most things work out, and if you are open to a little serendipity, you can come across some amazing experiences.

One such experience occurred that year, February 29—Leap Day. My wife and I were driving out in the country and saw a sign that read "1.5 miles Spectacular Sculpture." This was out in a rural area surrounded by dairy farms.

Odd as it was, if the sign had read "Ordinary Sculpture," we probably would have ignored it. Something about someone declaring their work "Spectacular" intrigued us. We followed one sign and then another. Over hill and dale, we went. Passing countless farms in the bucolic countryside. We ended up doing a dozen twists and turns.

At one point we even had this story made up about them luring us in for the kill like in a horror movie. After 1.8 miles we found this long driveway filled with, as it turned out, spectacular sculptures. Not "a" sculpture but plural. The artist is amazing, and his work is on display all around our area. His name is Paul Bobrowitz of PBJ Spectacular Sculpture.

I shared this story with a friend who was so intrigued she reached out to the artist and bought some pieces from him. Never mind that the art was in Wisconsin and my friend in Whidbey Island, Washington. It took two years and some interesting logistics, but the pieces arrived at my friend's home and are on display in her yard.

I'm sure there were things we could have been doing at home that day. You know, important stuff like cleaning or laundry. Every once in a while, just embrace the serendipity of the moment. Doing so led me to a memorable Saturday drive and making connections with art and friends across the country.

Reflection

- What is something you've talked about doing but haven't done yet?
  - o What are the specific barriers keeping you from taking that first step?
  - o What is one small, concrete action you could take today to start removing those barriers?
- What interests you, now or when you were a kid?
  - o Reflecting on those interests, how many have become buried or forgotten over time?
  - o How might you intentionally reconnect with and explore those early interests?
- Describe a time when you unexpectedly stumbled upon something interesting or meaningful.
  - o How did embracing that serendipitous moment influence you?
  - o How might being open to similar unplanned discoveries create opportunities to experience Ikigai?
- Ruth Asawa's approach was to follow what interested her.
  - o How might adopting a similar attitude support your own Ikigai journey?
  - o What might it mean for you to let your interests, rather than a specific goal, guide the way?

The Path Ahead

In these past two chapters we've moved from theory into practice by applying these ideas and methods to uncovering your Ikigai. Now you are ready for the next part of the quest. The journey of a thousand miles.

12

The Journey Begins. . .

"The journey of a thousand miles begins with a single step."
—Lao Tzu[1]

A JOURNEY OF any kind starts with a single step. Whether it ultimately ends a thousand miles later or eight hundred sixty-six. If you think 866 is an unusual number to end on, you are right. It is not the number I had in mind in January 2023, starting my fifth running journey of a thousand miles in a single calendar year.

This is the journal entry written after my first run toward those thousand miles.

My nose was congested to the point each breath was an exercise in determination. The sun had abandoned me behind the clouds, winds howled, and the cold invaded my bones.

It was the first run of the new year and even with the cold, it felt good to move. To experience being outside and running for the first time in weeks.

Even though I set an intention to run 1,000 miles each year, it is not a goal in the traditional sense. Goals are essentially made up, with little to no understanding of the future as we create them. We invent them out of some hope or wish of how we want the future to go.

131

Yet, we can't predict or control the future, which makes setting goals almost useless. In prior years, I've set an intention to run 1,000 miles in the calendar year. That's a long way to go. It requires averaging 2.74 miles each and every day of the year.

That's why it is framed as an intention because it's not a goal. It's not a have-to kind of thing. The desired outcome is to stay healthy. Running regularly keeps my body lean and fit.

Without those 1,000 miles out there as an ambition, it is easy to take a day off and then another and then another. Knowing every day without running leaves me 2.74 miles under 1,000 motivates me to get off the couch and on the road.

As a former engineer, it won't surprise you that my mileage is tracked in a spreadsheet. January 1st this year I entered the 3.5 miles into the spreadsheet, marking the first run of my 1,000-mile intention. Then my eye caught the "Miles to Go" column.

996.5

Since I've reached 1,000 miles four different years, you'd think it would be a piece of cake mentally. Even with the many successes behind me as I approach the current calendar year there is some trepidation.

For a split-second looking at that number generated a fearful thought taunting me about the enormity of the task. Then I reset and reminded myself that only the next mile matters. I don't have to do 1,000 miles at all, let alone right now. Focusing on my outcome instead of a goal frees me to drop the fear and keep going.

Prior 1,000 Miles Journeys

I've completed four calendar-year 1,000-mile running journeys. Each year presents its own challenges and opportunities for growth and reflection. In 2020, I didn't think there was even a remote possibility. I was recovering from Covid where I couldn't even walk a mile for months, let alone run.

I kept running even when it was hard, and I was terrible at it. The Kaizen "terrible" version can be applied to anything, even an individual run. After months of terrible runs I began to wonder if I'd ever be able to run again. Still, I kept going day after day, no matter how slow or terrible, putting in the effort.

By July, I realized that I had recovered and put in enough training that maybe, just maybe, I could hit the mark. In the waning days of December, on a lonely country road with wild turkeys crossing in front of me, I passed 1,000 miles. It was as much a spiritual journey for me as physical, pushing through doubts, failure, and illness.

This Time It's Different

The next year, 2021, was going to be different. At the close of 2020, I had fully recovered from illness and would begin the new year at my highest fitness level ever, as rated by VO2Max. It was going to be the best running year of my life!

Then, unrelated to running, I injured my neck and missed eight weeks. As I mentioned, to hit 1,000 miles in a year, you must average 2.75 miles daily. Missing eight weeks put me over 150 miles behind pace.

My Focus Word for 2021 was **intention**. I learned the value of intention and acceptance in that running year. Through disappointment and frustration of injury, I ran with intention and acceptance. I kept at it while allowing for proper rest and for days when the body or lungs weren't ready for a long run.

I permitted myself to have "terrible" runs and even not to make 1,000 if that was how things went throughout the year. In late December 2021, on a beautifully sunny and deceptively cold day near Pewaukee Lake, I passed 1,000 miles.

Year of Creative Running

Thankfully, 2022 was injury and illness-free. My Focus Word was "create," and it was a year of creative running. The cold air in our Wisconsin winters triggers my asthma, forcing me to run on a treadmill many days. I consulted with my doctor on a strategy to create healthy conditions to control my cold-induced asthma while running outside. We came up with a plan, and that year there was no treadmill running—every step was accomplished outside for the first time, even on the coldest days.

Outcomes Over Goals

The 1,000-mile intention gets me out and running. Having an outcome of health rather than a goal of miles keeps me going while encouraging me to allow time for rest, recovery, and life's inevitable surprises.

Toward the end of 2023 I caught a cold that progressed into pneumonia, forcing me to miss over a month of training. If I had a goal of 1,000 miles, the old me (before Ikigai) would have pushed myself to run, stressing myself out over closing the gap. I would have run before I was ready and in conditions that risked my health.

Even before pneumonia, I was behind the curve much of the year because of some bizarre stretches of extreme cold in the spring and sizzling weather in the summer of 2023. There were many days when it wasn't safe or in support of my outcome of better health to run.

After recovering from pneumonia, I Kaizened it, starting slowly, running short distances, working my way back to shape and health. At one point, while out on a run, I did the math and figured if I ran 6 miles a day every day until the end of the year, I could still make 1,000 miles.

Six miles was my pre-illness daily distance. As I made the mental calculation, I could feel myself increasing pace, running faster. Then in a moment of clarity I shortened my stride and slowed my breathing. The goal-driven perfectionist Dave of the past would have kept that increased pace. The harmony-focused Dave of today enjoys running for the sake of running and embracing the outcome of health.

On what turned out to be another cold day, the last rather than the first of 2023, my journey ended 134 miles short of 1,000. It was the first time I hadn't achieved 1,000 miles in any year I set it as an intention, and it was okay.

One Small Step

You'll notice many elements of Kaizen in all those 1,000-mile journey stories. No matter the circumstances, the path to success is to frame the challenge in the smallest increment possible. Certainly, in a 1,000-mile quest and sometimes even on an individual run, I will tell myself I only have to run the next mile.

Once I reach that mark, I commit only to running another mile, and so on. I typically finish six miles when the weather is nice, even on days where one mile seems enormous at the beginning.

Systems and Practices

Kaizen is an essential to our uncovering work. Another is to set up systems and practices that support accomplishing what we set out to do.

For my running it's getting enough sleep, regular rest, equipment, and time. I reserve a big enough window of time in the day and in the year to achieve 1,000 miles.

By stretching myself with this landmark, I've forced myself to learn how my body works. It is clear to me how many consecutive days I can run without a break and factor that into my mental planning.

I can tell when I'm tired and need rest. I've also learned the signals when pushing myself harder is in order. None of that came overnight. Part of understanding ourselves comes from doing things. In stretching ourselves and exploring, we learn what we are made of and what we can accomplish.

A practice supports growing that understanding of self. A practice is not just a simple habit or routine. It is an intentional act that adds richness and value to your life. It can be as simple as taking a few deep breaths every morning or as complex as a daily yoga or meditation routine. The key is that you choose to do it consistently, with purpose and mindfulness.

Utilizing a practice creates a sense of structure and routine that can help you stay grounded and focused. Approaching your practice as a ritual can also give it a deeper meaning and significance beyond just going through the motions. The Seven Rituals of Calm are terrific examples of this.

Moreover, framing your practice as an exercise that challenges you to grow and develop over time can help you become the best version of yourself. I invite you to find a practice that resonates with you, commit to it consistently, and see how it transforms your life. It's a way to connect with yourself and the world around you. Such a practice can create a sense of continuity and flow amid the chaos and complexity of daily life.

You may not be a runner and, even if you are, most aren't inclined to run 1,000 miles in 365 days. That's okay, everything shared are meant to be models of an approach.

Sitting at my desk finishing writing these paragraphs, I see the sun is coming out—time to lace up the shoes and head out the door. This run is going to be fun.

Reflection

- What in your life right now seems like a daunting task? Even if it is something you want.
- How can you break it down into the smallest possible step?
- What little thing could you do to start moving toward that outcome today?
- How might you set up a system to support you in this?
- What practices and rituals can you incorporate?

As we conclude the second invitation, it is an opportunity to reflect on the Uzumaki. You will recall the Uzumaki swirl (see Figure 12.1) represents the process of creating and refining your Ikiverse as well as your understanding of Ikigai.

Starting on the outside, our understanding moves ever inward, refined, tightened, and made deeper. Your uncovering process is never complete in the same sense of the Shaker approach to perfection. Perfection as being the best you can do today or in this application, perfecting your understanding.

Figure 12.1   The Uzumaki Swirl.

Using your Ikiverse is much like this. You will start at a point on the edge with your first version of Ikiverse. As you use and live into it, traveling the path of the spiral, your understanding will be refined; you will narrow in on a progressively vivid image of your Ikigai.

The preceding chapters have been examples of exploration and reflection using your Ikiverse as your model for uncovering. Though this process is ongoing, what you've learned up to now will serve you in accepting the next, the third, invitation.

PART

III

The Third Invitation
Living Out Your Ikigai

13

Harmony

I SPECIFICALLY SELECTED the word harmony over balance for the definition of Ikigai because balance has these connotations of equality. People will talk about work–life balance as if work and life are either separate or equal. Instead, harmony should be our goal. To understand what it means to live in harmony, let's go deeper into the distinction with balance.

harmony: (n)

1. agreement; accord; harmonious relations.
2. a consistent, orderly, or pleasing arrangement of parts; congruity.[1]

The root "ar" in harmony means to fit together. From both Latin and Greek, *harmonia* it means agreement or concord. Concord further speaks of agreement, union in opinions or sentiment, state of mutuality, friendship, and amiability.

Risk

If we take the musical meaning it is easy to see why harmony is what we should seek. The discord and noise prevalent in our modern world are the antithesis of harmony, leading to disagreements, discord, and disturbances instead of beautiful music.

Achieving harmony has become elusive, as the noise of the default disrupts our peace and prevents us from living a life of integrity. Beyond the noise in our lives, attempting to balance distorts our priorities. While many seek "balance" such as work–life balance, it creates a false equivalency.

It implies *work* is half and *life* is half. It becomes more about time management than living out your true essence. Life is not meant to be compartmentalized into rigid halves; rather, it should revolve around uncovering and living out our purpose in whatever we do.

The focus becomes compartmentalizing "you" into different buckets and boundaries and allocating time.

Opportunity

Embracing harmony means aligning passions with purpose, infusing every moment with meaning and joy. Living in harmony allows us to live out our purpose whether at work, spending time with loved ones, or even grocery shopping.

All aspects of life blend seamlessly, like a symphony. Different parts of life may rise and fall in importance, each playing its role at the right moment, creating a dynamic composition.

Sometimes work may take the lead, and other times, family or personal interests may shine brighter. Ikigai embraces these fluctuations.

Let harmony resonate within, allowing the interplay of different elements to blend into a harmonious whole. This leads to a more fulfilling experience where authenticity and purpose unite, creating a symphony of joy that echoes through every note of life.

Application

Ikigai is about experiencing your essence and purpose in harmony with whatever you do.

At its root, harmony is about the pleasing arrangement of parts and congruity. That's all well and good. How do I apply this, you might ask? Look for simple opportunities to bring harmony into what you do throughout your day.

Here are some ideas for small things to start doing right away:

- Eat slower.
- Ask questions.
- Read something new.
- Make mistakes and learn.
- Be okay with not knowing.
- Spend some time with nature.
- Teach someone something you know.
- Remove the worry of what others think of you.
- Sprinkle in simple pleasures throughout your day.
- Learn something *you* don't know by reading or asking questions.

Give one or more of those a try and embrace the peace that comes from living in harmony with your purpose.

When building practices and habits, choose harmony over content. By aligning the things you enjoy with the things you do, you find harmony and connect with your Ikigai.

- The best book is the one you can't put down.
- The best fitness activity is the one you relish doing every day.
- The best healthy food is the one you find delicious.
- The best work is work that creates flow, which is most like play.

Ikigai is meant to be easy. Living it out is something you do as part of who you are and why you're here. If it takes a lot of effort, it likely isn't Ikigai. Now, you might be saying, "Well, I had to create my Ikiverse and do all these other things. That wasn't easy." And yes, absolutely, there is work in uncovering and then some work in exploring. The actual experiencing of Ikigai is intended to be easy, connecting in flow, in harmony. It's experiencing your life purpose at the truest essence of yourself in everything you do.

Going from the default life to a life of purpose is a big change. As Buckminster Fuller noted, "You never change things by fighting the existing reality. To change something, build a new model that makes the existing model obsolete."[2]

Reflection

- Reflect on the moments of your life when you've had peace. Where all parts of your life were working in accord.
    o What were you doing?
    o Who were you with?
- How might you incorporate more moments like these into your day?
- Which areas of your life do you feel the least harmony?
    o How might you have fewer moments like these in your day?
- When have you felt like you were enough, that you had the love and acceptance you needed?
- Envision a life of harmony aligned with who you are at the deepest levels.
- What small steps can you take today to move closer to this vision and make it a reality?

The language of default became the normal path for a reason. A change to be a change must transform things or make them better. Saying something needs to change is fighting an existing reality. It is better to make the old system, in this case the language of default, obsolete with an obviously better system. It's not a change if you can't sustain. If we can't sustain, we can't keep the gain.

Any life transformation must be sustainable, and the only way to do that is to express your essence and purpose in harmony with whatever you do.

Life Smacks You in the Face

"There are years that ask questions and years that answer them."

—*Zora Neale Hurston*[3]

Harmony sounds great when we are talking about things we enjoy doing. How about maintaining harmony when life smacks you in the face? In 2015 I experienced every high and low and unharmonious event you could imagine. It was one of those years where life hits you with everything. It began with nothing but questions and ended with the first hints at some answers.

In January of that year, I visited my father. After retiring, he would winter in Arizona, and as was my practice I would fly out from Wisconsin to spend a week with him. My stepmother had passed away the year before, so it was just him and me.

As we watched a sunset together one evening he mentioned he enjoyed just sitting and being together with me, which is what we did. Not a lot of talking, only being. That entire week was that way. Whether we were hiking in the desert or sitting and watching the sun go down, we connected like never before.

Without planning to do so, we were on a quest to know and experience one another. At week's end, we hugged and said our goodbyes. As he turned away, I pulled him close one more time and kissed him on the head like I did when I was a boy. "I'm glad you're my dad. I love you."

"I love you too," he said. It was less than a week later that he was gone. He was a complex and imperfect man, and he was my hero. I miss him.

Six weeks later, my first grandchild, "E,"[4] arrived. A month and a half after E's arrival, my youngest child, my daughter, graduated from college.

A few months after her graduation, on the hottest August day in Wisconsin history, I gave my only daughter away in marriage. Following the honeymoon, she and her new husband moved to Chicago, and she started law school.

Then I turned 55. In my career I was leading a large Continuous Improvement Transformation program at one of the most storied companies in the world. Years before I had convinced them that despite the success the company had enjoyed, it could be even better. The CEO was visionary enough that he didn't want our company to end up like so many, falling into stagnation and irrelevance by being unable to adapt and innovate.

I literally took this from the seed of an idea to a pilot program to prove the concept all the way to building it out and leading it. The transformation helped change the company culture to an innovation focus and created hundreds of millions of dollars in productivity savings.

For years, my performance reviews had been progressively better as well as my bonuses. My evaluation that year, after our biggest successes ever, was a so-so "good job" keep doing what you are doing disappointment. No bonus, no raise, and no projection of growth. Only months before, the CEO shook my hand and publicly congratulated me in a companywide ceremony.

I sat down with a friend and mentor of mine who was an executive vice president at the company and said, "Hey, what's the deal here? I've created this successful program at a company that already thought it was great and made it even greater. I handed them all this money; the CEO congratulates me in front of the entire company and now I get an *okay* review?"

He said, "Well, I'll tell you, but if you tell anyone what I said, I'll deny it." I said, "Okay, fair enough." And he proceeded to reveal that I had aged out. There was an unwritten rule about a 10-year window where you had to be promotable twice within that time, or you couldn't be promoted at all. I had reached the end of that window. "I can't get promoted anymore because I am too old to get promoted twice?" He replied, "Yep."

He went on to explain that while this rule wasn't written down anywhere, it was baked into how many of the company's leaders thought and acted. My bosses and their peers all followed it like it was set in stone. This unofficial rule had become as binding on my career as any formal policy.

I had to look in the mirror and ask what I was going to do because I loved the job and the people. Now, not only would I not receive any promotions, with the system of pay brackets in place I probably wasn't going to get any more raises either.

This realization forced me to invest in some soul-searching to determine what this meant for me in terms of my Ikigai. We always have the choice in response to such treatment, to become bitter or better. It would have been easy to devolve into being bitter. There is nothing more inharmonious than bitterness and anger. Ikigai enables us to choose better.

I landed on two approaches. First, I didn't sit passively and instead began actively looking for other jobs. I had a lot to offer to a company and many ways to impact lives through my work of making things better; I didn't have to remain where they no longer valued me.

The other approach, however, involved deliberately aligning my focus and intention on the best ways to consciously live out my Ikigai in my current role.

If there's one thing in my life that I've consistently enjoyed pouring my heart into, it's making things better. People, process, product, systems, and so on. In each case, I get energized about making whatever exists today better.

My part in growing the program while advancing my career had essentially come to an end. With the energy previously invested in those activities now available, I redirected my focus. I began looking for opportunities to make things better outside of my explicit role while continuing to act with integrity and earning my paycheck.

I carved out a new mission separate from the transformation itself, focused on codifying the cultural change that I had been leading. I began sharing that learning through my writing. Then I studied design at Cornell and began coaching and mentoring other leaders in Design Thinking as well as doing individual mentoring. All of these activities brought me back to the core theme of my Ikiverse: encouraging, empowering, and enabling people.

I also started knocking off a little earlier in the day. Again, acting with integrity in terms of doing the "job," but not the extra stuff. Outside of work I used the newly free energy to redouble my efforts to connect with my family, friends, fitness, and self-reflection.

Of Endings and Beginnings

One wonders how you can hold the feelings of happiness and sadness at the same time. That entire year was a weird amalgam of merriment and melancholy, joy and sorrow, loss and gain, endings and beginnings.

August seemed to be the peak of such a time. My daughter's wedding was filled with both joy and sadness. August has had many such moments for me these past many years.

The most recent significant August event was in 2023. The Wisconsin State Fair ended, and with it, summer for most. School starts soon after the fair ends.

It also marked the end of an almost nine-year journey for my wife, and that began unexpectedly in 2015. Early that year we thought we were becoming empty nesters for the first time since our oldest son was born.

My daughter, our youngest, was away at school and in her final year. She'd be home only briefly in the summer before, as I mentioned earlier, getting married and moving to Chicago for Law School. Instead, our daughter-in-law threw us a curveball that became one of the greatest gifts I've ever been given.

Our first grandchild had arrived, and Caitlin asked if we'd be willing to watch him three days a week when she returned to work. This was right in the middle of my year of questions and answers.

There hasn't been a happier moment in my life than holding "E" for the first time. Becoming a grandfather was an extra blessing after losing my father. Still, this request produced some conflicting emotions.

My wife was struggling with multiple sclerosis. Her energy was often drained from dealing with her symptoms. Adding in caring for a baby would certainly tax her already low energy reserves. Not to mention, our time together as empty nesters would come to an end before it began.

A New Dream

There was a commercial[5] a while back where a guy retires and finally has the means to buy his dream car, a vintage Datsun 280Z. Unexpectedly, his son gets a job transfer, and his granddaughter comes to live with him to finish high school.

Though he loved his granddaughter, her presence disrupted his life, plans, and finances. Over time the joy of having his granddaughter with him helps him forget his initial frustration, and at the end of the commercial, he hands her keys to a new car. "Wait . . . Grandpa, what about your dream car?"

"This is my dream now," he says, handing her the keys. Mine was a similar journey, minus the dream car.

First came "E," who stayed with us several days a week, and then his sister "C." For a while in 2023, we added granddaughter number two, our daughter and son-in-law's first baby, "S," to the mix. Pouring love into them became my dream. Instead of time taken away from things I wanted to do, it became a greater opportunity to express my essence and purpose in harmony with caring for them.

Now, years later, as the state fair ended, so did summer and with it that chapter of a dream. Both of the older kids will be in school full-time. They won't be staying with us regularly. We've added our daughter's second child to the mix, our grandson "M," who through no small irony was due in August. They have a stay-at-home dad and so we don't watch them as regularly as we did the first two.

"One wonders how you can hold feelings of happiness and sadness at the same time."

I wrote that in my journal the day after my daughter's wedding, which also happened in August. My corporate career ended in August with an early retirement and similar mixed emotions.

Repeatedly, August seems to be a mix of sad endings and hopeful beginnings. It has been nice not to be stepping on Lego pieces left after a day of play. I've gotten more time to write and get some things done around the house. At the same time, even now, I am barely able to write this, thinking of not having them here as often.

Plenty of inharmonious events have occurred and yet by applying the lessons of Ikigai they became blessings and opportunities to live out my calling in far more profound ways than making an already prosperous corporation even more so.

While my grandchildren don't need as much time caring for them, I have far more energy to devote to extra time doing things with them.

Harmony Over Balance

You can see examples of looking for harmony throughout all of these 2015 events. Looking to balance them would have taken me down a different path altogether.

Like the symphony, where different parts of life may rise and fall in prominence, each plays its role at the right moment. Rather than fighting the existing reality, I built new models for my work, for my life at home, and for my personal growth and development that made the existing model obsolete.

In searching for new jobs, I looked for opportunities that would allow for harmony with my new reality. Looking back, virtually none of the jobs I interviewed for would have been supportive of my new model. It may come as no surprise that none of them worked out.

Several times I was in the final stages of negotiation, having already been selected for the role, when something completely unexpected and often bizarre would happen. In one instance the executive vice president of a large well-known global company had picked me to lead a major company transformation. At the last moment, the board of directors changed the job requirements from "experience working with India-based companies" to "experience working in India."

While I had managed many teams based in India as well as relationships with many Indian consulting firms, I had never physically worked in India. Suddenly I was no longer eligible for the role and the offer was withdrawn. A year later they still hadn't filled the job.

Looking back there is no way I could have embraced my role of "grandpa" in the way I was able to if that job worked out.

Any life transformation must be sustainable, and the only way to do that is to express your essence and purpose in harmony with whatever you do. I continued to look for job opportunities while remaining open to a new reality that was better and would replace a life of corporate jobs.

Solomon said, "To everything, there is a season and a time to every purpose under the heaven."[6] In each of these examples, a season was passing, and a new one is beginning, replacing the existing reality with something more aligned with my purpose.

"Our life is a short time in expectation," said Henri Nouwen,[7] "a time in which sadness and joy kiss each other at every moment." Never more for me than in 2015.

14

Hara Hachi Bu

LIVING OUT YOUR Ikigai is the third invitation, because it builds on the first two. Applying what you learned to get the noise down and uncover your purpose constructs the foundation for a life of meaning. As we learned in the last chapter, expressing who you are at the deepest levels and why you are here, all in harmony with whatever you do, is living Ikigai.

Which, naturally, brings us to the philosophically profound topic of . . . candy bars. Imagine you are eating your favorite candy bar. It can be whatever kind you like best. Removing the wrapper your mouth waters in anticipation of the first delectable taste. You take a bite and savor the flavor in your mouth. Now stop!

In that first fabulous bite, you received 70% of the flavor sensation and taste you will get from the entire candy bar. It's called sensory adaptation and applies to how our body perceives sensory input.

In this case our tongue is surrounded by an abundance of flavor. Each subsequent bite reduces the response the body makes to the taste sensation. The more you experience a flavor, the less intense it becomes.

Leaving a Little on the Table

When I was a boy, we rarely had dessert and even more rarely something out. One time my grandmother gave me money so that I could buy an ice cream sundae on my walk home after school.

She inadvertently gave me enough to buy two so when I finished the first one, I thought a second double scoop hot fudge sundae would be even better. It wasn't. By the time I finished the second I regretted wasting the money because it didn't taste nearly as good as the first. Back then I chalked it up to a "bad" sundae, though now I know it was the process of sensory adaptation.

Back to the candy bar. You've had your first bite and experienced the majority of the flavor sensation while consuming a third of the calories. Think back to Kaizen. The key to Kaizen is reducing feelings of fear or being deprived.

Because you've only eaten a small portion, if you were to stop now you might feel deprived. Even if you logically and correctly told yourself the remaining bites would have almost no value while adding empty calories.

What if instead you broke the candy bar in half, keeping one piece and giving the other to a friend? Now when you ate your half you would feel like you "finished" your candy bar. You'd have enjoyed closer to 90% of the available flavor, consumed half the calories, and wouldn't feel like you deprived yourself of enjoyment.

If you had eaten the entire candy bar with the ever-diminishing flavor, you would have preset your mind for a reduced level of enjoyment in anticipation of the next time you open a candy bar wrapper. Because you ate only half, your last taste was still high sensory value. You left a little on the table to desire for your next candy bar.

Leaving a little on the table is the idea behind hara hachi bu. It is rooted in Confucianism and is the principle of eating only "8 of 10" or 80% rather than eating until completely full. We've all eaten a meal where afterward we were so full we could barely move. Much like our candy bar example, any meal like that had diminishing flavor value the more we ate.

This isn't about weight loss, though the practice of hara hachi bu contributes to healthy eating. It is no coincidence that ancient practitioners settled on essentially an application of the modern 80/20 rule.

When we connect it to Ikigai, hara hachi bu goes beyond eating less to a focus on better experiences. Remember, most of the good things in life come from a small amount of the inputs. There are few things of value; focus on those things, grow those things, and make those things better.

As the great designer Dieter Rams advised, "We want to make things better. What we need is less, but better."[1] The idea being that we need less and we need what we have to be better. There is a strong application of this principle in our Ikigai journey.

- Less stuff and the stuff we have, we need to make better.
- Doing fewer things and doing them better.
- Fewer "connections," better relationships.
- Better experiences, fewer things.
- Less work, and the work we do needs to be better.

Even the things we want or need, need to be better. This promotes harmony in all we do. Applying that to food, we need less food, and the food we eat needs to be better. We need less food, and the experience of enjoying it needs to be better. More on "less" and its application in later chapters; for now, let's focus on eating.

Being so full that we can't move isn't living in harmony with our needs for food or health. Mindless eating plays into this as well. A while back I was watching a basketball game on television and grabbed some cookies. I had eaten two of the three before I even realized what I had done. I'm certain I wasn't hungry, simply doing mindless eating with my attention on the game and not even enjoying the cookies I had eaten.

When we slow down, we can be more intentional about what we eat. There is nothing wrong with an occasional chocolate chip cookie. If I had thought about it though, I would have waited until after dinner to eat anything and might not have even desired a cookie if I ate a satisfying meal.

Savor

Slowing down our eating allows us to savor each bite. To savor something is to taste, breathe in, appreciate, and enjoy wholeheartedly.

Imagine savoring a meal versus what I did, eating two cookies and not even remembering having eaten them. I'm not sure what to call that though it is certainly the opposite of savoring.

Application

My grandkids and I were making fresh sourdough bread recently. The aroma of bread baking filled the house. Taking the loaf out of the oven, the smell gently rose and touched our noses with a tangy sourness. After it cooled a bit, "C" tapped the top of the loaf. The hollow sound it made confirmed the bread was done.

I sliced it down the middle so both kids could touch the inside, experience the texture, and smell the now stronger aroma. A pat of grass-fed butter slathered across the first three slices and we were ready to taste.

"E" likes a dollop of natural honey on his. The amber liquid mixes with the melting butter. Each of us then in turn took a bite of our slices. The best sourdough makes your salivary glands tingle inside your cheeks, which is exactly what all three of us experienced. Letting each bite slowly dissolve in our mouths extended the enjoyment.

That is savoring your food. We reveled in each moment from making to eating. It would have been easy to devour that bread, and certainly part of the enjoyment is eating it while it is hot. Still, by taking time and intention to savor we multiplied the value of our experience. We also didn't need to eat a dozen slices, as eating slowly allowed our stomachs to fill naturally. The satisfying taste also contributed to feeling full. Though we could have eaten more, we didn't, because we were satiated with taste and volume. Less . . . but better.

There was also a personal connection. The three of us enjoyed a shared experience. The kids talked about how much they enjoyed making and eating the bread the rest of the time they spent with my wife and me that day.

Easy Ways to Incorporate Hara Hachi Bu

The next time you sit down to eat, start small. Take a small bite and experience it completely. Notice the texture, the flavor, the change in both while the bite of food is in your mouth. Eating can become a complete and harmonious experience. You'll notice as you do this your satisfaction level goes up and your desire for more diminishes.

Avoid things that make you feel deprived. Much like with the candy bar example, when we eliminate feeling deprived, we enjoy the food we do eat more while eating less of it.

Plate size is an easy way to eat less while not feeling like you are giving something up. People tend to want to "clean" their plate. I know growing up my parents pushed for me to eat everything on my plate. I still fight feeling like it is "wrong" to leave any food uneaten.

This is where serving food on a smaller plate helps us to naturally eat less. We still get the psychological satisfaction of finishing everything on our plate, consuming fewer calories while still feeling like we've had a complete meal.

This principle can be applied when eating out where you can't control the size of the plate. If you get a to-go box and put half in at the start you get a double win as you "finish" what's on your plate, getting that satisfaction while saving the other half for another day.

Much of our eating is emotional. Learn to pay attention to why you feel like eating. Ask yourself:

- Are you hungry?
- If not, what emotions or needs might be triggering the eating?
- How do you feel before, during, and after meals. What are your emotions?

Becoming aware of why you eat will help you embrace hara hachi bu and avoid overeating outside of meals times as well.

Making a Change

Let's put embracing changes like hara hachi bu in a Kaizen frame. While it's tempting to go all in on something new—and I understand that urge—changing a habit is best done through small, incremental steps. The "small" can be adding or changing only one habit. Don't start running, change your diet, take up mediation, and try to learn a new language all at the same time.

Adding only one new behavior or making only one change each month still results in 12 major changes a year. For incorporating hara hachi bu into how you eat, try one of the things I mentioned earlier or one of these:

- Don't eat after 8 p.m.
- Cut back on the sugar you add, a little more each day.
- Eat at home most nights during the week.

One small change per month means a dozen over a year. This adds up to big change over time. Because the change is slow and easy, and you don't feel deprived, it's change that's likely to last.

More Than Food

While the original application of hara hachi bu centers around eating, the idea of 80% full can be applied to all other areas of our Ikigai.

Take running, for example. There are days when I feel like I could run forever. Yesterday was such a day. Cloudless sky, mild temperature, and little to no wind. My legs were strong, lungs clear, and the sun felt warm and soothing on my skin. Passing the six-mile mark as I neared my home, there was a longing to keep the feeling going, tallying a few more miles. Instead, I stopped.

My legs were still felt fresh and would be ready for my run the next day. I wanted to keep going. By leaving a little running undone I made space for running another time. Had I run eight miles there is a chance I might have overextended myself. The next day, slightly stiff or my muscles tired, I might have skipped a day or, worse, run full out again and drained my body even more. By running only 80% full I enjoyed my run and set myself up to enjoy the next run.

It's a great way to leave things just to the point of satisfaction. Whether eating, working out, playing a sport, or learning a new skill, it's always good to have something to come back to tomorrow. It keeps the learning and experiences a lot more enjoyable.

We do something similar in Lean Transformations in processing or manufacturing where we leave a "little work" to do the next day to start the production line, priming the pump, so to speak. This leads us to the concept of efficiency, whose typical application is utterly at odds with the principles of Ikigai. That is what we will examine next.

15

Efficiency

LIVING OUT YOUR Ikigai is not a life hack or productivity play centered on efficiency. A focus on efficiency and productivity will lead you away from the fulfilling life of Ikigai. Many people will ask me, "Dave, you're a globally recognized productivity and efficiency expert yet Ikigai isn't about either of those things. How do you reconcile the two?" Maybe you are wondering this as well.

Applying the 80/20 rule by growing the vital few things in our Ikigai space leads to a more efficient and productive life. While true, those benefits come about as a byproduct, not by making that the initial focus. Allow me to explain through a story.

The Red Rotary Phone

During the early days of my final corporate role, I initiated a company-wide transformation program by leading several small Kaizen pilots. The director of one of the call centers reached out to me, excited because she wanted her team to be one of the first I worked with.

I asked what problem she felt she needed to solve. She answered, "We need to reduce average handle time." I asked her why and she answered, "We've got to become more efficient."

In a call center, average handle time refers to the amount of time on the phone or holding the phone receiver handle. Call center people

157

today wear headsets, and it is a linguistic anachronism to say handle time, but it has stuck around.

On my desk, I keep a red rotary dial phone, which was over 50 years old even then. "Oh, if average handle time efficiency is your goal, I can solve your problem right now," I said, and I picked up the receiver handle of the vintage phone.

"I'll write work instructions for your operators to answer the phone and then hang up immediately," I said, placing the receiver back down. "You'll have zero handle time. Actually, not quite at first. There'll still be a second or two as they hang up. Eventually, though, the customers will quit calling and you'll be at max efficiency. Have I solved your problem?"

She answered me in less than polite language. I laughed, and responded, "Well, let's talk about it then." I asked more questions and learned that whenever a customer called, the call center personnel were typically on the phone helping them for about five minutes.

Digging deeper I also uncovered that on average, customers had to call in three different times to get the right answer. This meant three 5-minute calls for a total of 15 minutes of combined time on the phone, or what is referred to as contact time.

Even though hanging up immediately is an absurd thing, you can use an absurdity like that to test whether you're thinking makes any sense or not. I explained to this director that when you start with efficiency, you get solutions like hanging up quickly to get off the phone faster.

Clearly, the solution wasn't about getting off the phone faster because you could do many things to achieve that. Get the operators to talk faster. Have them respond to questions with any answer to get them off the phone. Or the extreme and absurd idea of hanging up immediately.

I suggested an alternative. "What if instead, we doubled the average handle time?" This resulted in an even greater exasperated response from her. "Hear me out. Your total contact time is 15 minutes. If we doubled the handle time, but answered the question correctly in 10 minutes, you've reduced your total contact time by a third." Then I had her interest.

The key thing is that if you start with efficiency, you do things like try to get off the phone quicker. Rather than efficiency and productivity it is best to adopt another Japanese philosophy, Lean.

The Foundation of Improvement

Many people think of Lean only in terms of manufacturing. The first thing that often comes to mind is Toyota, who has used Lean manufacturing to produce a full range of vehicles, from economical models to luxury cars, all known for their exceptional quality and reliability.

Lean is about much more. Though it is most commonly linked to continuous improvement in business, there's an application for us in our pursuit of purpose. Lean is built on foundational principles that align remarkably well with living out your Ikigai.

Two operating principles of Lean center on removing waste and adding value. When you remove waste in your process, in your product, or as we've been exploring in this book, in your life, you gain capacity in terms of time, money, energy, or focus.

Reinvesting the capacity you gain from waste removal creates the virtuous cycle we talked about in previous chapters. Reinvesting it in value add is when wonderful things happen.

Identifying and strategically removing waste was exactly what I did with this call center director. I started with a question. *Why do people have to call in three times?*

I devoted time to connecting with her team to understand their jobs and challenges in order to learn the answer. What I found was because of a lack of experience, training, and documentation the operators often didn't know the answers.

Rather than take a hit on their performance evaluation by spending handle time to research the answer, they gave any answer they could come up with to get off the phone quicker.

This kept average handle down, improving the perception of efficiency. It also resulted in the customer having to call back in again. And again. When you start with efficiency as a goal you get bad behaviors like this.

Little by little I identified where all the waste was in their process and determined the root causes. The biggest waste was wrong answers. They were caused by lack of documentation, training, and experience. The situation was exacerbated by the urgency of getting off the phone.

No small irony was the high turnover in the department due to low employee morale. People don't enjoy jobs where success is impossible. High turnover led to new people with no experience and to training issues. Lack of experience led to more wrong answers. It becomes easy to see the flywheel moving in a negative direction creating a vicious cycle of self-perpetuating waste.

I began working with the team on ways to reduce waste, which would allow them to focus their time and energy on adding value. Nearly 80% of their customer issues could be solved by knowing the answers for 16 products and services that represented approximately 20% of the products and services this team supported. The 80/20 rule in play again.

In one case, 40% of the calls could be answered by understanding only four products and procedures. Simply updating the documentation by experienced operators for those four most common types of calls resulted in a significant drop in repeat calls.

Customer satisfaction went up—value add for the customers. Operators were helping the customers, and their job satisfaction went up—more value add for the employees. Ultimately the average contact AND handle time went down—value add for the company. The director eventually got her efficiency as a byproduct of waste removal and a focus on adding value.

Two Pillars

The other part of Lean that I connect with Ikigai is the Two Pillars— Respect for People and Continuous Improvement. While the operating values of waste removal and adding value are foundational to Lean, the two pillars represent its philosophical core tenets and depth, strongly connecting to living out one's Ikigai.

Respect for People acknowledges that our time is limited. Wasting someone's time disrespects them as a person. For example, asking call center operators to rush through calls while ill-equipped to address customer questions shows no respect for their time or ability to find success in their roles. We were asking them day after day to work a job where there was nearly no opportunity to achieve any level of success. Similarly, making customers call multiple times for the help they need demonstrates a lack of respect.

Respect for People goes deeper—understanding that we all have limited time on this Earth, and a purpose to realize. Our interactions with others should respect that limited time and the value each person brings by living their purpose or Ikigai. Respecting people means valuing their ideas, empowering them, and creating an environment where they can find meaning through their work.

The Continuous Improvement pillar links back to the Shaker ideal of always investing in being the best "us" that we can be. It's not that you're *bad* today and you've got to get better. It's that perfection, as the Shakers said, is acknowledging the best we can do today. Then recognizing what we do tomorrow might need to be a little better. Investing in learning and understanding about ourselves in such a way that we become the best us that we can be.

That's why the self-help and life hack approach is not aligned with Ikigai. Life hacks are all about efficiency and productivity. Again, when you start with efficiency and productivity, you get wrong behaviors that ultimately don't even lead to efficiency or productivity. You get a water-saving toilet that uses 30% less water per flush but has to be flushed twice to actually work.

Start with understanding the foundational elements of life: our essence, why we're here, along with the methods and means to live those out more effectively. This will get you efficiency because you won't be spending your time in your 80% that's waste. See, I told you we would get back to 80/20.

Instead of wasteful activities, we take that time, energy, and resources and invest it in the 20% that is 16 times more valuable. You are investing in that 20% when you are living out your essence and your reason for being here in harmony with whatever you do, your Ikigai.

Become Zealous

I want to encourage you to become a zealot. By zealot, I mean to be singularly focused, fervent about applying the 80/20 rule to your Ikigai.

Remember, few things matter. Find those things, focus on those things, and grow those things. To live out our Ikigai, we have to find that 20% where the majority of our joy, our fun, our enrichment comes from and grow it.

To live a wonderfully fulfilled life, every moment doesn't have to be in our 20% space. Again, this is not about maximizing efficiency, getting every moment of every second of every day to be exactly this, or productive, or any of those kinds of things. Instead, it's about looking for opportunities to remove the waste in your life and replace it with value. To respect yourself and others—honoring time, commitment, and unique gifts.

Then continuously invest in improving so that you are living out your Ikigai in every aspect of your life as much as you can. Remember, a 1% change in your Ikigai space—your vital 20%—is worth 16 times more than time spent in the wasteful 80%.

Delete the Line

Here's a real-world example of being zealous about guarding your time and avoiding waste in your life. It also happens to be one of my favorite examples of standing up against corporate bureaucratic nonsense.

This story takes place during a phase in my career when I was heading up the network team for a large IT organization. We were having some budget problems, and our leadership decided that they were going to track every single dollar in our budget.

There were 40 managers in this department. Senior leadership decided that we'd have to document everything we were doing down to $10,000. These were $20–$40 million budget segments. In such a large budget, $10,000 is a rounding error.

I was running a support team at the time, and support has sort of got to be done one way or the other. Whether you classify it as a project or break fix, the work is still the same thing. Even so, my bosses wanted me to document whether I spent $10,000 on support or $10,000 on projects or $10,000 for something else.

Making this classification was irrelevant because my budget was fixed. It was going to be what it was because I needed so many support people, no matter how you cataloged it.

That year, I reluctantly did the budget segment process. Every time I was off even slightly, I had to have a meeting with three or four people and explain it. I'd be off $10,000 in one direction one month and it would even out by being $10,000 off the other direction the next month. Nevertheless, both resulted in meetings and a waste of time. By the end of the year, I was within a few hundred dollars of my planned budget.

Also at the end of that year, we did nothing with the results. Nothing. No decisions were made, no analysis taken, no value determined for any of this "budget management." Naturally, senior leadership announced we were going to do it again the next year.

I'd had enough. Right there in the middle of the meeting announcing this repeat strategy, I asked, "Why are we doing this and what are we going to do with the feedback since we didn't do anything with it this year?"

The guy running the meeting looked at me, aghast that I would ask such a thing. He also had no answer other than we had to do it to "manage" the budget.

I wouldn't let it go, insisting that we needed some justification for the investment of time in an activity that produced no results in the prior year. My concern was duly noted along with a few scowls, and the meeting proceeded with planning the budget-tracking process for the coming year as if I'd never raised the concern.

Back in my office, I sat down, frustrated at the prospect of wasting so much of my time for another year. Then it hit me.

We tracked everything in a spreadsheet. The manager leading the effort would put a master spreadsheet online and I'd fill out my projections. It would be those projections he would use to track against my actual spending.

My first question was, what if I don't put in my numbers? If I do put my numbers and they are off, then I would have four or five meetings. But what if I don't put them in at all? If I don't put them in, they'll see zero and that will trigger a meeting.

What if there was no line to see? What if I deleted it? If there is no number, it will cause an alert, but if there is no line, there is nothing to check. There were 40 managers in this division. I wondered if they would they even notice if I had deleted the line?

So, I did. I deleted the line, and they didn't notice. Six months later, I was having lunch with a colleague, and he was complaining that he had to go to one of the budget meetings because his numbers were off for the month.

"I've got a meeting with the Bobs," he said, a reference to the movie *Office Space* and dealing with consultants. "What about you? How's it going with managing your budget and the Bob's?"

I made him promise not to tell anyone and then said, "I deleted the line."

He threw his hands up in the air all but shouting, "I can't believe it." He said some other things that a former Army guy would say to a former Marine that I won't print here. You get the idea.

Eliminating Waste

Throughout my career I would do things like that to get back some of my time. Instead of wasting my time on worthless work, I'd eliminate it. Using the time I saved not doing worthless stuff, I invested in my team, my personal growth, in helping other managers, in making our products and our support better. It is a big reason I was able to advance in my career. In the "delete the line" example alone I saved five hours a week over each one of my peers. That's nearly six weeks of reclaimed time over the course of a year. Imagine what you could do with that much extra time.

When you understand what charges you and what drains you, it becomes easier to identify waste and be zealous in efforts to remove it. I'm a zealot about removing wasteful and unproductive activities like budget tracking with no purpose.

Zealot might sound extreme, though it is an appropriate word because it takes an intense commitment to pull it off. Not only must you focus on removing waste, other people will do everything they can to pile more things on to you. It's just the way life is. For some reason, that's especially the way the world of work operates. You must zealously guard yourself and your time by offloading as much of that kind of worthless activity as possible.

Despite holding executive roles at several Fortune 500 companies, moving up the corporate ladder was never my ambition. My pursuit was autonomy—owning more and more of my time. The further up the organizational chart I moved, the fewer people could dictate how I spent my days. While it may have been perceived as ambition, my sole desire was to be left alone, free to immerse myself in the work that energized me. The more I could safeguard my time, the better. Titles and offices paled in comparison to owning my time and devoting it to what mattered most.

Not Defective in Any Way

It takes a tremendous act of courage to admit to yourself that you are not defective in any way whatsoever.

—Cheri Huber[1]

In the world of Continuous Improvement, where I spent decades of my life, the word defect plays a significant role in eliminating waste. A "defect" is anything you don't want to have happen. Going to our earlier example of the call center, a customer receiving the wrong answer when they call in is a defect.

Equally, a second call that provided the right answer to that same customer would also be a defect. While the answer was correct the second time, the defect lies in the fact that a second call was necessary at all. If you are struggling with that concept, you are not alone. Much of my teaching and coaching as a Continuous Improvement consultant is spent helping people understand this idea.

We don't like defects or being defective. It's a tough word to accept even when it doesn't apply to us and even more so when it does. Here's some good news.

You are not defective in any way. You don't have to be improved, optimized, productive, or efficient. You are a perfect creation even if that perfection is buried under layers of lies, disappointments, and other debris life has thrown at you.

You, at your essence, are a pristine soul untouched by setbacks, sorrows, judgment, and pain. That exquisite untouched spirit is who you are and were always meant to be … peaceful, confident, brave, and true.

That's why Cheri Huber's idea speaks to me and why you may have difficulty believing the preceding paragraph. While we wince at the word defective, we simultaneously can't accept the idea that we are defect free. We can't accept that at our essence we are perfect just as we are.

In Psalm 139, King David explores the idea that in our innermost being we are all "fearfully and wonderfully made." The Hebrew word for fearfully, in this passage, is "yare," which means crafted with great respect, honor, and reverence.

Most are familiar with the early life of King David as it played out in the well-known story of his battle with Goliath. Yes, it is *that* David. He was brave and even at a young age destined for leadership. In Jewish and Christian scripture, David is referred to as a "man after God's own heart," though he was anything but perfect.

A historically recognized and renowned king, David abused his power, was a dysfunctional husband and father, and even faced attempts on his life by his own son due to family conflicts. Despite these glaring imperfections, David demonstrated a remarkable capacity for self-awareness and repentance, recognizing and atoning for his failures, flaws, and sins.

It is against this backdrop of human imperfection that David's words in Psalm 139:14 (NIV) take on profound significance: "I praise you, for I am fearfully and wonderfully made . . ."[2] Here is a man keenly aware of his own shortcomings yet affirming the inherent perfection and worth of our unique creation as human beings.

David's acknowledgment of our inherent worth and beauty is all the more validated precisely because it comes from one who could be considered among the least perfect of people. Someone who had stumbled and sinned greatly nonetheless recognized that, in our inmost being, each of us is fearfully and wonderfully made by our Creator.

King David provides a great example of how we can operate in our Ikigai space. We can recognize that we have things that could be worked on while simultaneously accepting we are defect free by design. At our innermost being we are still yare, a being crafted with great respect, honor, and reverence.

Improvement in Service to Ikigai

I gain a few pounds over the winter like I often do in part because I run less. It is typically five pounds though this past year it was over 10. I will lose that weight though it won't be because there is something wrong with me and needs to be fixed.

Part of living my Ikigai is being healthy so that I can experience my essence and purpose in harmony with whatever I do. For my health, I will embrace activities aligned with who I am in harmony with my life. That might mean running more or enjoying fewer cookies.

It won't mean running on days when I need rest or creating conditions where I'll feel deprived, that is, no cookies at any time until I fix this weight problem. There is no problem to fix in me because I am defect free. Even the thing I want to address, my weight, can be tackled by living and expressing my Ikigai.

When we quit trying to "fix" ourselves we learn to "be" ourselves. In no small irony, many things we see as defects that need adjustment are changed by operating in harmony with whatever we do.

Much like starting with efficiency and productivity, seeing ourselves as defective and in need of fixing leads to bad behaviors that don't "fix" us anyway. Seeing ourselves as inherently beautiful leads us to behaviors that help us "be" that person more fully.

Let's continue the weight example. When I carry a little more weight, it is no big impact to expressing my essence and purpose in harmony with whatever I do. If I don't deal with it and add more weight beyond a certain point, my breathing is more difficult, which impacts my prayer and meditation practice. I don't have as much energy to be present for wife, my kids, or my grandchildren. My running becomes more difficult and puts more stress on my joints. I go from a state of harmony to disharmony rapidly.

If I want to express the true me, the one who is fearfully and wonderfully made, I need to address my weight. Not because I am defective, but rather so that I can live fully into the non-defective creation that is me.

It is an important distinction to make. You are defect free and there are conditions that support you living fully into that creation.

It is okay to address those conditions in service to your Ikigai and true self.

Reflection

- Why does it, in the words of Cheri Huber, take a tremendous act of courage to admit you are not defective in any way whatsoever?
- Take a moment and imagine yourself as perfect just as you are. How does that feel? Do you believe it?
- How differently will you live your life as someone "fearfully and wonderfully" made?
- What is one small thing you could do today to embrace that perfect inner essence?

Free from the drive to "fix" ourselves, hustle, or be efficient, we can now pursue a healthy approach to "better," which is where we kick off the next chapter.

16

Better Next Year

BY NOW YOU'RE seeing a pattern emerge of how to experience your essence and purpose in harmony in whatever you do—your Ikigai. It's built on the three invitations:

- Getting the Noise Down.
- Uncovering your Purpose.
- Living out your Ikigai.

What you may also be noticing is that the practices, rituals, experiences, and learning you get in each invitation support the next invitation and are ongoing throughout your life. My story from Chapter 15, "Deleting the Line," about the budget, illustrates how all three invitations play out in real-life situations.

Living Your Ikigai

Living our Ikigai is an ongoing effort of getting and keeping the noise down. The Seven Rituals are just the beginning. They provide the platform and the foundation and your mindset. As with all things Ikigai, the process starts small and then is applied over and over again. Being zealous about eliminating waste is vital because noise represents waste in your life. Deleting that line in the spreadsheet was a huge noise reducer.

Understanding Your Purpose

As you progress, you'll continue refining your understanding of your purpose. This involves uncovering and recognizing those moments where your true essence is revealed—what energizes you, what gets you going—and applying your Ikiverse time and again.

In my case there's nothing about my Ikiverse, my purpose that supports doing budget work in general, let alone the worthless budget work when I decided to "delete the line" instead. Knowing that helped me identify work that drained me, and applying the Getting the Noise Down techniques helped get rid of it. Aligning your actions with your purpose and reducing the noise in your life sets in motion a self-reinforcing cycle of growth and fulfillment.

The Virtuous Cycle

Reducing the noise of the budget work led to my career success, and similarly reducing the noise will give you the capacity for reinvestment that starts moving the flywheel, ultimately creating the virtuous cycle and opportunity to live out your Ikigai. Each application of the invitations builds upon the last, creating momentum.

Remember Uzumaki. Like the swirl, our journey starts on the outside and moves ever inward, refined, tightened, and more profound. Your first experience with this was creating and then experimenting with your Ikiverse. In our journey we are always learning, growing, and gaining wisdom.

Application

Uzumaki is very freeing, giving us the peace of mind that we don't have to have all the answers today, and we'll always be on the path of getting a little bit better and ever closer to living our Ikigai.

Even so, we tend to need some levels of delineation and demarcation of progress. We innately respond to certain moments that mark the passage of time, whether it's a fresh start of a new week, a month, or a year. These are known as temporal landmarks.

Temporal landmarks are dates that have a significance that separates them from our ordinary days, and which separate a past period from the present moment or future. They help draw a boundary between one period in our lives and another. Research suggests that they can help provide motivation for change, giving us a fresh start. That's why New Year's resolutions are so popular. More on that in a bit.

A New Beginning

Temporal Landmarks provide a spark to start again. We can mentally consign our old selves to the past, detaching our image from our mistakes and imperfections.

Adam Alter and Hal Hershfield coined the term "9-enders"[1] for people in the last year of a life decade. Those who are 29, 39, 49, 59, and so on. When people near the arbitrary end of a decade, something stirs that often alters their behavior.

While first-time marathon running participation drops off after the age of 40, it shoots back up dramatically at 49. In fact, a runner is three times more likely to sign up for a marathon at 49 than at 50. It is an example of the drive a temporal landmark can provide.

In my own case I ran my first marathon at 57 (not 59), though looking back I had that arbitrary marker of turning 60 in my mind when I decided it was time to run one. Because they provide markers, temporal landmarks strongly influence our perception of time. They often provide inspiration for reflection.

Another powerful marker of time is your birthday. Birthdays provide a significant temporal landmark for several reasons. First, it's a unique personal moment; it's your birthday after all, not the beginning of the new year for everyone. It's yours. Like most temporal landmarks, birthdays prompt reflection on the past year and spark future aspirations.

A birthday encourages us to reflect on the things we've done, the challenges we've had, and how much growth we've had over the year. It also inspires the setting of new dreams and new visions for how we might be better next year.

Like any temporal landmark, birthdays can act as that fresh start, giving us a clean slate, which can be motivating. Unlike other temporal landmarks, that clean slate feeling is uniquely personal because it's your day.

Better Next Year

New Year's resolutions are often dramatic declarations of change that almost always fail. We've learned from applying Kaizen that fear or feeling deprived often prevents us from making a change. Think about the sense of deprivation you might associate with losing 50 pounds, or the fear triggered by setting a goal to run a marathon when you've barely jogged around the block.

We often set huge New Year's resolution goals and give up early in the year. In fact, by the second Friday in January, often referred to as "Quitter's Day," most have abandoned their ambitions for change. It is the enormity of these resolutions that sets us up for failure. Our brain immediately activates those feelings of fear, judgment, and deprivation that are the barriers to meaningful change.

To combat this tendency to quit, let's instead employ one of the most powerful Kaizen practices by doing something small. In this case asking a small question. Here is one of the most potent small questions you can ask on your Ikigai journey.

"How might we. . . ?"

How might we see improvement in our lives without triggering fear of change or anticipating the pain of deprivation? Clearly not by making lots of change at once. The Kaizen approach keeps fear and feelings of being deprived down by making small and lasing change.

How might we use Kaizen and temporal landmarks to move us closer to living our Ikigai? What would be a small change we could make using a temporal landmark? How about better next year or on your birthday?

Better can be small and cover any part of our lives. It keeps fear down without having explicit stretch goals attached. Your birthday gives you a personal temporal landmark and gauge. It is like receiving permission to start over fresh and new and be better by the next time you celebrate your special day.

Before we move on, I want to address a question that's going to come up with at least some of you when you think ahead to using your birthday as this landmark. What if my birthday is only a few months away?

One of my favorite clients has been Sue.[2] When I first introduced Sue to the idea of using her birthday as a refresh point, she got completely hung up on the idea that her birthday was only three months away so she couldn't make any significant change in such a short time. I encouraged her to do a reframe of "better next year."

As with everything I teach in Ikigai, these are examples, frameworks, and ideas and none of them are set firmly in stone. You can always give yourself permission to do something that's different which meets you where you are at this point in life.

For Sue, I encouraged her to go ahead and set the "better by her next birthday" and give herself three extra months to do whatever *better* meant. Now she had 15 months. She liked that because it gave her the new start feeling of her birthday temporal landmark and was Kaizen enough in terms of enough time to eliminate her fear.

Again, temporal landmarks are completely arbitrary things that we've created—the beginning of a week, the beginning of a month, the beginning of a year, a birthday. They're also powerful devices to help us focus. Use them to help you focus while not letting it be any kind of hindrance or resistance.

Better next year is a helpful way to make change and progress in your life. Remember from the last chapter, you aren't defective in any way. Better in this sense simply means more aligned with who you are at your deepest levels, expressed in harmony with whatever you do.

One reason I push back against the overly career focused Venn Garden is how it makes "be"ing harder. Ikigai is not supposed to be hard. Becoming a better or more aligned reflection of the real you should be easy.

I love counterintuitive things for their power to create dramatic change. There is nothing more counterintuitive than your ultimate calling and destiny being easy. Easy to uncover and easy to express.

Trying Not to Try

One counterintuitive idea I initially struggled to understand was wu-wei (woo-wey). While wu-wei literally translates from Chinese as "no trying," some describe it as "effortless effort" or "trying not to try." Trying not to try is a term coined by author Edward Slingerland[3] in his book of the same title.

If you are in wu-wei you aren't doing "nothing"; you are acting in something like a state of flow. You might be creating art, writing, running, or other things without strenuous effort. We often link "trying" or "effort" to things being hard.

Trying hard requires a lot of energy and can be exhausting. We are typically tense when we are trying or working hard. Wu-wei is about being relaxed. Of course, relaxing and trying hard seem like completely contradictory things. How might we bridge that contradiction? What if we explored trying hard in a relaxing way?

Trying Hard Easily

The concept of effortless action is admittedly perplexing at first glance. As with most profound ideas, a relatable example is the best way to illustrate it. Let's explore this concept through a simple exercise that combines focused attention with relaxation.

Find a comfortable seated position, allowing your body to settle in. Gently release any tension by placing your awareness on different parts of your body. Start with your head and slowly move down to your neck, shoulders, back, and so on. As you bring your attention to each area, consciously release any tension and allow it to relax. Breathe deeply and easily, allowing a sense of peacefulness to envelop you.

Once you feel relaxed, continue reading. As you read, pay attention by focusing on the words while remaining aware of your relaxed physical state. Notice how you're engaged in an intense activity—reading and comprehending—while also feeling calm, peaceful, and relaxed. This is the essence of effortless action: being fully present and active, yet without strain or struggle.

Allow any outside thoughts to come and go without getting caught up in them. Notice how you can maintain focus without having to "work hard" at suppressing other mental activity. This balance of engagement and ease is at the heart of effortless action.

This state of effortless focus might feel familiar to you. In fact, you've likely experienced it before. You've probably settled into this state of relaxed focus while reading a favorite book—the kind you get so immersed in that hours slip by without you even realizing it.

That is wu-wei . . . effortless effort.

Trying not to try seems counterintuitive, and it is, of course, which is why it is so powerful and a pivotal behavior to living into Ikigai. Some link the concept of wu-wei to flow, and while there are elements of flow that align with experiencing Ikigai in this way, there are important distinctions.

Flow, as described by psychologist Mihaly Csikszentmihalyi,[4] refers to the state where one becomes completely immersed in an activity, operating with focused intensity while feeling energized and fulfilled. It arises when there is an optimal balance between the challenge of the task and one's skills to meet that challenge.

For flow to be sustained, the activity must continually ramp up in complexity and demand ever-greater mastery. There is a constant striving for new levels of performance that push the boundaries of one's abilities. Flow follows an upward spiral of taking on greater challenges to achieve more intense states of absorption.

In contrast, wu-wei-oriented Ikigai is not predicated on perpetually growing complexity. Rather, it is about aligning our actions with our reason for being—our essence and purpose. The aim is to live and work in harmony, not to constantly transcend previous levels of performance or achievement.

Think back to the Shaker definition of perfection. The best we can do today. That is perfectly aligned with wu-wei as Ikigai.

The pursuit of flow can become something driven by ambition. Remember being disconnected from our Ikigai is an integrity issue as in an integrated self. A lack of integration leads to disintegration. In contrast, Ikigai expressed as effortless effort aligns with becoming ourselves rather than a constant striving for more. Ikigai involves a settling into one's core purpose. It is less about achievement and more about embracing harmony in everything we do.

Saturate and Sit

One way I incorporate effortless effort into my life is a practice I call Saturate and Sit. When grappling with the "big" questions or seeking insights, I begin by fully immersing my thoughts in the reflection—saturating my mind with it.

Then, I walk away for a while, allowing the seeds of connection and insight to settle into the soil of my unconscious mind. After taking a break, I return to sit with the question again for a brief period. Repeating this process over many days if needed.

Our minds often need time to work through their natural processes organically. Trying to force insights will likely only yield superficial results. These multiple sit-down sessions allow the depth of sustained introspection required. Those seeds of insight planted earlier begin to grow into a greater understanding.

One of the most pressing questions I've employed this technique with is around the concept of striving. "What if I stopped striving? What would it mean? How might life be different?"

Strive means making great efforts to achieve or obtain something. I've always been a striver. Invariably, the next milestone, next goal, next achievement—we think of striving in relation to success and achievement. The root origin of the word is decidedly different and stems from meanings like quarrel, dispute, resist, struggle, putting up a fight, and attack. Not harmonious at all.

To give you some idea of how my reflection went, assume for a moment that after years of struggle, you stopped all the striving, hustling, and trying to push forward. Instead, you rested and looked back on the journey of life so far. Whether the past is good, bad, or somewhere in between, you begin seeing yourself now. From this state of awareness, you acknowledge what has been and who you are with grace and acceptance.

Then imagine you are standing on a beautiful shore with a new invitation. You are drawn to the surprise of the new horizon. Life is now ready to complete whatever has been left undone up to now. The you that has always been there is ready to be expressed in everything you do. That's the beautiful state of mind I came to as a result.

Sitting with it multiple times is like co-designing with two great minds. Each session contributes a new idea or insight to the more extensive design. A single session alone doesn't provide the space and time to let the answers to big questions percolate. When I make space for this, it almost happens by itself.

In Harmony

Harmony in music is pleasing to the ear. It settles us and gives us peace. Harmony requires an absence of absolutes. You'll notice so much of Ikigai is about creating a sustainable approach as opposed to explicit rules, directions, or steps.

We experience the harmony of Ikigai in everything we do when we . . .

1. Minimize wasteful resistance and struggle.
2. Align with our nature and the unfolding of life's circumstances.
3. Allow our actions to be expressed effortlessly from intrinsic motivation.
4. See perfection as the best we can do today.
5. Define better as a greater expression of our essence and purpose.

Achievement and flow are excellent examples of something that if overemphasized creates noise, discord, and disintegration. Properly incorporated into life, they add to our harmony. Activating your Ikigai often requires engaging activities that allow for periods of flow. The difference is that those flow states are in service to expressing your purpose in ever deeper and richer ways as opposed to embracing escalating complexity.

Similarly, achievement can be in service to Ikigai in terms of learning, growth, and fulfilling a calling. Where we get into problems is when achievement drifts into a state of striving. That's why framing both around the concept of wu-wei and applying them to Ikigai is so transformative.

Being you should be easy. Being your authentic self should come easily. The principles of "Better Next Year" and "Effortless Effort" offer inherently harmonious approaches to living in alignment with your Ikigai.

Even as we learn to live in a state of harmony and connection to purpose, one of those "thou shalt" scales can reappear when we least expect to disrupt our path to Ikigai. Next, we will explore the dangers of drifting into striving.

Reflection

- What temporal landmark in your life feels most significant to you? How might embracing this moment as a fresh start change your perspective?
- If you truly believed that "better" simply meant aligning more closely with your essence, how might that transform your approach to personal growth?
- Recall a time when you experienced effortless effort or wu-wei. What made that moment special, and how might you invite more of those experiences into your life?
- How does the idea of "trying not to try" challenge your usual way of approaching challenges? What might change if you embraced this concept?
- If you were to stop striving and instead focus on expressing your true self in everything you do, what would that look like in your daily life?

17

Playing Games

I DIDN'T REALIZE when I had my dream about being done it was essentially about striving. I talked in the previous chapter about my personal reflection on striving using the Saturate and Sit approach. While that was an excellent example of a reflection technique and the connection to effortless effort, it was not the whole story of striving.

You cannot live your Ikigai if you are in a state of striving, period. There is simply no way to be fully engaged in any spiritual practice if you are in a state of striving. Remember the root of striving is about quarreling, resisting, struggling, and attacking.

Where Does Striving Come From?

When we are young (*some of you still are*), we set career goals and aspirations. Those are fine and a natural part of our growth and development. We have a position or an amount of money in mind that will make us "happy" or satisfy our needs.

That ambition, like any, leads to another and then another. Think for a moment about how that process starts. It's almost a game. We play lots of games in life, and the games start early.

- As a young child, you're playing the **school** game or playing the **social** game.
- When you start to work, you begin playing the **money** game which at some point transitions to the **status** game.

179

Each of these games has progressively longer time horizons. Eventually, perhaps you are at this stage now, we come to realize these are not real life at all, just games.

We must ask ourselves . . . If it is just a game, does the outcome matter? Don't you get tired of games? I did.

I'm at the stage where I'm not only tired of games, I also want something more from life. I want to live out why I was created, expressed as my true self and essence, in harmony with everything I do. That is the life of Ikigai.

It is very much the two halves of life question. Even the first half of life portion where we go to school, build relationships, marry, create a career, and more can be lived without playing the game by the rules the world tells you to play.

There is a reason Jesus admonishes his disciples, "I tell you the truth. It is very hard for a rich person to enter the kingdom of heaven. I'll say it again. It is easier for a camel to go through the eye of a needle than for a rich person to enter the kingdom of God" Matt 19:23–24 (NLT).[1]

Not because being "rich" is a bad thing. It is easy to get hung up on the word rich. In the passages just prior to Matt 19:23–24, Jesus was asked by a young man what it takes to enter the kingdom of heaven. He answered to live a right and just life by not stealing or murdering, and by loving your neighbor. The young man answered that he had lived by all these commandments and wondered what else he lacked.

Jesus told him, "If you want to be perfect, go and sell all your possessions and give the money to the poor, and you will have treasure in heaven. Then come, follow me" Matt 19:21 (NLT).

The young man responded by walking away in part because, the passage points out, he had many possessions. He was saddened by the request because he was playing the game of striving. It wasn't that he literally had to give up anything material. The meaning in Jesus' admonition was to stop making those possessions the most important thing and live the life you were called to live.

Much in the way Confucius taught wu-wei as a state where your actions spring forth effortlessly from your inner virtue, moral development, and alignment with your reason for being. There is nothing effortless about striving, focusing on more and more.

*There is no way to be satisfied when you only want one thing,
and that one thing is more.*

At various points in my life, I have achieved a level of success.
Every time I've been stressed or unhappy since my dream about being
"done" has been when I was unwittingly striving instead of living
my Ikigai.

A Punch in the Arm

It was October and technically winter uniform regulations for Marines
were in effect. This meant the sleeves on our camouflaged utility uniforms were unrolled, buttoned down, and covering our arms.

This was Naval Air Station (NAS) Memphis located just outside
of the aforenamed city in southwestern Tennessee. The sun was scorch-
ing and it seemed there was more than 100% humidity squeezed into
the hazy air.

It was the beginning of a long stay in Memphis, and as part of my
check-in I dropped by the Navy Credit Union to open an account.
Enjoying the welcomed relief of air-conditioning, the teller and I made
polite conversation and then I asked if it was always like this in October, thinking it was abnormally hot.

With a slow, southern drawl that could have melted butter, she
answered, "Ohhhhh nowa, it is yew-zhuh-lly muuuch waaah-mer
than this-us."

Exiting the building, the breeze hit me like opening the door of a
blast furnace. I could hear someone yelling off in the distance.

It was a Gunnery Sergeant, and he had two new arrivals standing
at attention. "I don't care what the regs say, it's 98° and 110% humidity. This isn't boot camp, you're Marines now. We expect you to use
your heads for something other than a place to put your cover (hat, in
Marine talk). Roll your sleeves back up before you get heat stroke." He
used some other words I skipped, though you probably get the idea. I
promptly went back into the bank and rolled my sleeves up to summer
regulations level.

NAS Memphis was where all Navy and Marine Corps aviation
technical training took place. My class started with 25,000 sailors and

Marines. Everyone took basic electricity and electronics, affection-ately known as bee double e.

The top people in that class went to several more increasingly challenging courses until, if you made it that far, an elite group of 20 people were then selected for Advanced First Term Avionics (AFTA). Those who made the cut for AFTA spent the next 20 weeks, 8 hours a day in class earning essentially an engineering degree in electronics.

We mustered up at zero five thirty hours (5:30 a.m.) and marched to class. Then it was class all day and studying all evening, hit the rack (go to bed) and do it all again the next day.

Entering the Marine Corps, I was 23, a little older than most, and had been married for several years. By the time I made it to AFTA we had a newborn. More than one evening I sat in the living room of our tiny apartment balancing a book on one arm and my infant son on the other. That was life for those 20 weeks.

I knew it was going to be a tough class to pass, let alone come out as the top student and be named the Honor Man of the class. If the Honor Man was a Marine, they received promotion to Corporal. Corporal in the Marine Corps enters you into the noncommissioned officer ranks. Along with it come significant increases in pay and opportunities for on-base housing and other financial benefits we des-perately needed.

Balancing a baby with the stress of intense training and regular Marine stuff thrown in, I wasn't sure I was even capable of completing the class, let alone finishing as the Honor Man. On top of that, these were the best of the best. To use a familiar analogy, it was like Top Gun for aircraft engineering.

Everyone got in by merit alone. Test scores and performance were the only measurement. There wasn't a single person there who didn't deserve to be. In my meditation and prayer the day before class started, I was reading Psalm 112. One verse stood out in particular.

"Their hearts are secure, they will have no fear; in the end they will triumph on their foes" Psalm 112:8 (NIV).

It reminded me I earned my way in and deserved to be there like all the other students. I also took the promise of triumph as an indica-tion I would do well. Passing was one thing, being first would require extra time and energy. Time and energy I wouldn't have for my wife and son. It would put a lot on her, so we made the decision together. Alicia and I prayed and decided I would give everything I had and if after the third week I was in first place I would go for Honor Man.

After week one, I was in third place, just a fraction behind first and second. In week two, I moved up to second place. And by week three, as you're probably going to guess, I was in first place. I decided right then and there, I was going for it. I wouldn't be in first place again for the next 16 weeks.

Petty Officer William Creighton[2] was a classic technology geek. His father had been an AFTA Honor Man years before. Creighton was well schooled in naval aviation culture and technology. Being single, living in the barracks, he had nothing to do but study. In week four he grabbed the lead.

Each of those weeks where I was trailing Creighton, I would remind myself, in the end, in the end, in the end, that was the promise, in the end. Doubt, not Creighton, was the foe I would have to triumph over.

Redoubling my effort, I gave it my full, focused energy. Not grinding away mindlessly—I put in quality, concentrated effort over a sustained period to get the job done right. Reaching week 20, it came down to the final exam, which was broken into two parts. The first was a comprehensive written exam. Creighton and I both aced the test.

The very last thing, with only hundredths of a point separating us, came down to soldering. Soldering doesn't seem like much of an engineering challenge, but on military aircraft, solder is weight. Weight can make a huge difference in whether a plane operates properly or not, especially in a combat situation.

We had an hour to complete five solder projects and on each of the first four I did well. The very last thing I had to do was place a connection tip on a coaxial cable, much like the ones used for cable tv or internet connections today. I had made dozens of perfect cables in practice all week.

For some reason, my soldering gun suddenly was not working properly. It wasn't getting hot enough and the solder wasn't running like it's supposed to. There was no time to ask for another soldering gun. The instructor would test the wire by trying to pull off the pin, and mine wouldn't stay on.

If they pulled the tip off, you lost 10 points. If the tip stayed on, but didn't look very good, you lost five points for appearance.

With time running out, I decided to put as much solder as I could on the cable to hold the tip and forget about what it looked like. That tip was not coming off no matter what.

With seconds to go I turned it in, knowing that I was hundredths of a point behind my competitor and with that five-point deduction had probably come up short.

As I turned to exit the lab I caught a glimpse of Creighton. He was struggling to get the metal tip to stay on his cable when time ran out. Creighton turned in his project to the instructor, who promptly ripped the tip right off the cable. After 20 weeks and hundreds of tests I became the AFTA Honor Man by 1/100 of a percent.

It sounds stressful, and while exhausting, it was anything but stressful. Once I realized I belonged in the class my confidence in my ability to do the study necessary to pass the course never wavered. I rested in my "in the end" promise to the extent that I didn't worry or expend useless energy. Again, I worked diligently though not hard in the grinding sense.

The class graduation included a formal military promotion ceremony. My newborn son wore an outfit made from a pair of camouflaged pants worn by me in boot camp. I had torn a hole in the knee, and they were no longer serviceable. My mother-in-law had made an outfit out of them for my now six-month-old son to wear to the promotion ceremony. She must have believed in me, as she made it well ahead of the ceremony.

Being promoted to Corporal, an E4, from a Lance Corporal, an E3, meant significantly more financial and other benefits, like access to base housing that we would need. I had gone into the military to provide a future for myself and my family. All of the work that went into this, all of the effort, was totally aligned with who I was, why I was there, and the people I loved. While there was pressure, the pressure wasn't a negative. As I said before, it was totally aligned with my Ikigai, though I didn't understand Ikigai at the time.

This alignment extended to my love for learning. Learning new things, competing, and testing myself in an environment like a classroom was part of my essence and purpose. I had always been very successful in school and enjoyed learning.

My intention was to come out of the service with tangible skills. The higher I went in the training like AFTA, the greater the opportunity for me and my long-term ability to take care of my family.

At the promotion ceremony, I was wearing my current rank, which was, as I mentioned, Lance Corporal or E3. I was promoted to Corporal at the ceremony.

The entire time that I was in this process, over a year, I told my wife, if I can just make Corporal, I'll be satisfied because I knew what that would do for us and for our lives in the future.

After the ceremony, we were standing around and people were congratulating me. Standing next to my wife, holding our son, my eye caught a Sergeant walking by in the hallway.

Now keep in mind, I haven't even worn Corporal stripes yet. I'd just earned them moments before. They haven't even been put on my uniform. But I saw a Sergeant and I said, "You know, I got Corporal early enough. I might be able to make Sergeant."

My wife reached up and punched me on the arm, half-joking, half not. That's the way I am, and it is perfectly aligned with my Ikigai. It wasn't stress and strain. It wasn't so much ego and drive. I'm always looking for the next thing to stretch myself, to grow. That is perfectly aligned with Ikigai.

Even though I was studying much of the time, I was still available for my wife and son, as well as the other requirements of being a Marine.

The difference between that and striving was the limited amount of stress. Again, there was the pressure of taking tests and studying, that kind of thing. There wasn't the added stress of pushing myself beyond the person that I was, my values, or the other priorities I had in life. Without striving, I avoided the disintegration that comes from trying to be someone or something I wasn't.

Because I was a Corporal, we were able to eventually get on-base housing, and it was a good thing as the next part of the story will reveal.

Aloha

With a year of the most rigorous and intense technical training in the United States military behind us, all that was left was to receive our "orders" as to where we'd go for our permanent duty station.

The Gunnery Sergeant stood quietly in front of the classroom as we waited for him to announce our fates. There was little surprise in store for me. My training was in electronic countermeasures, and most Marines trained in that specialty were assigned to Cherry Point, North Carolina. As the Honor Man, finishing first in my class, mine would be the last name read.

"Marlow," the Gunny barked. I stood and came to attention.

"You're going to Cherry Point for I-level training and then to," he said, pausing as he flipped the page, "Kaneohe Marine Corps Air Station, Hawaii, for permanent duty."

"Are you kidding?" I asked, falling forward, hands flat on the table in front of me.

The Gunny, a Vietnam combat veteran, shot me a look of disapproval and said, "Corporal Marlow, I don't, kid."

What are you going to Tell your Wife?

Even though I had been in the service for a year, being stationed in Hawaii would mark the first time we were more than driving distance away from family and friends.

My wife had moved all over the country growing up. Her dad worked for the government and was transferred frequently. All those moves had been made *with* her parents. Now, we had a baby with health problems, and she was going to be thousands of miles away from the only support she'd ever known.

I called immediately to break the news using the rotary dial payphone in the hallway. My fellow Marines stood close by, waiting to hear how the call went.

"We got our orders, and just like we thought, training will be in North Carolina. The permanent duty station is different. I'm assigned to Kaneohe Bay in Hawaii." To my relief, she was thrilled at the idea.

Growing up in Indiana, cornfields and basketball courts surrounded me; my first time on a jet had been only a year earlier traveling to Marine Corps Boot Camp.

Living in Hawaii was like being transported to another world. It was also challenging. While truly a paradise, the cost of living in Hawaii was way above my military salary. Renting while waiting for base housing was burning through all our savings.

Thankfully, base housing became available before we ran out of money. Again, that benefit was there because I had made Corporal. Here I was, a young military man living on the beach in the most luxurious place in the world. We embraced the entire experience as an adventure and were determined to get everything out of it we could.

Then about a year into our stay I began to lose my peace and dive headlong into striving mode. I had been selected for NCO—noncommissioned officer—school. As part of the requirement, I had to do an interview with the Sergeant Major of our squadron.[3]

The Sergeant Major and I talked career, family, and at some point, I mentioned that my wife was pregnant with our second child and was due anytime.

He decided that it was probably best that I not go to NCO school right now because there was a possibility she could have the baby early, causing me to have to drop out. The squadron only received so many slots for the school every year and he didn't want to waste one.

"I'll call Top Stern and tell him to nominate someone else this time," he said shaking my hand. "Good luck on the new baby, Marine."

I was relieved because there was a good chance that my wife would have our baby during the school, and our first son had a number of medical issues. I didn't want to be away or focused on school again like I was with our first child.

There was significant expense involved as well. It meant all new uniforms and other things that I didn't have the money for at the time. We loved every minute we were in Hawaii but the reality was it was expensive, and we had exhausted our savings waiting to move into base housing.

Master Sergeant Stern,[4] or Top for short, was new to our unit. I had built a great relationship with both my commanding officer and the prior Master Sergeant in charge.

In fact, it was the prior Master Sergeant who nominated me for the class. Top Stern, on the other hand, didn't know me and was immediately offended by the fact that a Sergeant Major called to let him know that he shouldn't be sending Marines with pregnant wives to NCO school.

Top Stern immediately summoned me to his office. In language I won't repeat here, he accused me of saying something to get out of the school, which I had not done.

I assured the Top of my willingness to return to the Sergeant Major and insist on attending the school if that's what he wanted. Top Stern dismissed my offer and declared, "I will ensure that you never make Sergeant and that your Marine Corps career is over!"

Up until that point the goal of becoming a Sergeant that started in the hallway right after my promotion ceremony had a normal level of priority. I took care of my physical fitness scores, my proficiency scores in work, all the things that went into getting a promotion. Now somebody in my chain of command who was supposed to support my growth and development was committed to actively stopping me from advancement.

That's when the striving began. Initially, I responded to the unfair treatment by voicing complaints to others. I became preoccupied with worrying about my scores and a myriad of unproductive, energy-draining thoughts. These thoughts not only wouldn't lead to my promotion to Sergeant but weren't the right reason for getting promoted. Worse, they drained my energy and negatively impacted other areas of my life.

I was suddenly experiencing all the negative things that I have warned you about concerning striving. One of my mentors, a Staff Sergeant who had been my sponsor when I first arrived in Hawaii, sat down with me to talk it through.

He heard me out as I ranted about a litany of reasons why the situation was unfair and wrong, and how enraged I was at Top Stern and everything else. After patiently listening, he posed a question that changed everything: "Dave, do you intend to make a career out of the Marine Corps?" I responded, "No, I enlisted to serve, receive training and education," explaining I was attending college at the time with plans to eventually leave the service and get an engineering job to support my family.

He looked at me for a second and asked, "Then why do you care?" That's when it hit me. I didn't care. Whether I made Sergeant or not wouldn't dramatically alter my life one way or the other. I was striving because somebody was trying to take something away from me, and I was fighting back to get what was mine.

Realizing that I wasn't looking to make a career of it anyway, the tension left, my shoulders dropped as I relaxed.

Striving and pushing and arguing and complaining and whining. Everything I was doing was in opposition to living out my Ikigai. There was no harmony in any of this.

Do Something Right

When my students are spinning out of control or clients in business have a mess on their hands, I often advise doing something right. Anything, even a small thing, done right or for the right reasons will begin the calming process and start the flywheel moving in the direction of a virtuous cycle.

My "do something right" after that conversation with my mentor was to focus on doing things that were good for me. Things that would set me up for success if an opportunity came about because it would have been nice to be a Sergeant if only for the accomplishment.

As I expressed before, I am zealous about the 80/20 rule and began looking at all the things that went into the promotion. We received points for how well we did on fitness, marksmanship, and our overall performance in our job.

When slots for promotion are available, which wasn't all the time, there is a cutting score. The cutting score simply meant that among all the corporals in the Marine Corps in this line of work, everyone at or above this score gets promoted. Everyone below is "cut" from promotion consideration.

I began doing things to help my cutting score and do it wisely with no striving and maintaining my focus, especially with another baby on the way. My fitness and rifle scores were already maxed out. My proficiency and conduct ratings, similar to a performance review in a civilian job, were where Top Stern had the biggest influence, possibly costing me several hundred points.

Time in service and time in rank were additional factors in the Marine Corps promotion system. You received five points for every month you had been in the Marine Corps (or service) and five points for every month you had been at your current rank. My early promotion meant I didn't have many points for time in the service. Though getting promoted early was a great thing, it did leave me way behind my peers in terms of the number of months of service points.

There was a way to make up for the lost points few people took advantage of—Marine Corps Institute (MCI) correspondence courses. This was in the days before the internet. For each MCI course you completed, you received 10 points. I decided to start doing the MCI courses.

You could do six at a time. I know this is probably hard for some to relate to, but there was lag time in the mail. You requested the course, then it would take a week to arrive.

You studied the material, then took the test in front of a proctor. Once that was complete you sent it to be graded, which took another week to get to Washington, D.C., then another week, sometimes more, for the points to be tallied.

Because of that, I had six going all the time. As soon as I finished one, I would request the next one. I was tallying an average of 10 points toward my cutting score every week.

This was anything but striving. Learning new things, studying, and, frankly, using the system and implementing an 80/20 strategy are all aligned with things I enjoy doing. It comes naturally, in harmony with what I do. I completely gave up the idea of being a Sergeant and simply did the things that eventually might lead to becoming one.

My focus returned to embracing and enjoying my time in Hawaii. My wife and I had set our intention to experience being in Hawaii as one big adventure. I was back to enjoying every single day we were there.

Without striving I also enjoyed time with my newborn baby, our second son, who was happy and healthy. Without the striving, my energy level was up and I was more present for my family. The focus was on enjoying things like the Honolulu Zoo and beach instead of stewing about Master Sergeant Stern in his vendetta against me.

I also kept doing good work in my job. Because of that, my commanding officer liked and respected me. I would learn later that as the cutting scores were announced, mine was the cutting score, which meant one point less and I would not have made Sergeant. But at 37 months in the service, when the average time to make Sergeant was eight years, I was promoted to E5, Sergeant United States Marine Corps.

My commanding officer, Major Mendes, told me later that because mine was the literal cutting score, he called the Pentagon to ensure that there were no mistakes and they processed everything just right.

On a beautiful sunny day in Hawaii, I received my promotion. As part of the ceremony, one of the senior people reads the promotion warrant or the promotion announcement. In this particular ceremony, Major Mendez selected Master Sergeant Stern to read my promotion warrant, announcing to the world that I was a Sergeant in the United States Marine Corps.

There's nothing wrong with wanting a career. There's nothing wrong with wanting promotions or more money or more opportunities, or advancement. The challenge comes in when we focus on that for either the wrong reasons or in the wrong way.

Though I didn't realize it at the time, my greatest successes came when I was true to myself. When I lived out my essence and purpose in harmony with everything I did, that's when I both found peace and achieved the most.

Quarrel, Resist, Struggle

Remember the root meaning of striving links to quarreling, resistance, and struggle. My initial reaction to being told I wouldn't be promoted at work because I was 55 was similar to my reaction to Top Stern.

I don't react well to authority telling me what I can and cannot do. Somewhere deep inside me, it's clearly rooted in some childhood things. I don't mean within the bounds of being morally upright or anything like that. I'm talking about in terms of accomplishment or what I can become or what I can achieve.

I've discovered anytime that happens, I'm at risk of striving because I want to prove someone wrong. Or I want to rebel against the system that is preventing me from being what I want to be.

Striving always leads to disintegration. Conversely, each time I act in harmony with my essence and purpose, trusting in a higher calling, good things happen.

When it came to being told I would never get promoted again at my last company, I began looking for other work. It was a constant striving activity, resume development, interviews, presenting or selling myself to others. Spending loads of money to get another job added pressure and stress when things didn't work out.

Things often didn't work out during this time in the most bizarre and unlikely ways. I can't even tell you how many times I came close to getting a new job, with many of them dream jobs in terms of roles and salary.

On three different occasions, we were in the final stages of negotiating an offer when something completely and totally unexpected happened that either eliminated the job entirely or eliminated my eligibility. Most of a year was wasted fussing, fuming, and fighting against those circumstances.

Things changed for me when I realized I was striving. Of course there's nothing wrong with looking for another job. There's nothing wrong with wanting to validate that your current employer is wrong about you or should be promoting you or any of those things. It was more the attitude and intensity that made it striving and wrong.

Instead of striving, I began looking for ways that I could expand my 20%, my Ikigai time. Expanding the opportunities to express my purpose in my current role, while continuing in a relaxed way, to look for other jobs. It was during this time that I got an unexpected opportunity to study design at Cornell.

Designing a New Life

Studying design proved to be a life and career-altering experience. For decades, I had delved into continuous improvement methodologies, but now bringing in human-centered design principles transformed me in ways beyond just enhancing my continuous improvement skills—it made me a better person overall.

A crucial aspect of human-centered design is the emphasis on listening. I had always considered myself a good listener when in reality I was always a willing listener. Learning empathy interviewing and other design techniques taught me how to engage in deeper conversations and become an effective listener.

Being a more effective listener impacted more than my career. It positively impacted my relationships with my wife, children, and, eventually, grandchildren. It literally changed my life, enabling me to live more fully into my Ikigai.

The primary reason I had the opportunity to study design was because I was actively seeking ways to expand my 20%, my Ikigai space rather than lament the ending of my corporate career.

Design also reignited my creative interests and energy. As a creative outlet I decided to start writing again. I had done plenty of writing in my career. This was different as it wasn't about work, promotion, a new job, or even to generate consulting business.

Writing this time was about expressing that part of me that for years had been hidden by discouragement, disappointments, losses, and the demands of everyday life. Through this process, I gradually uncovered that storyteller from Mrs. Huff's third-grade class.

When the prospect of early retirement arose, I found myself fully prepared for a new life. I had created my Ikiverse, exercised my creative muscles, and developed a newfound set of skills, desires, and passions. I was equipped to live even deeper into my Ikigai.

None of those new expressions of my purpose would have emerged if I spent those years pursuing the roles I had applied for, relentlessly climbing the corporate ladder.

Reflection

- Recall a time when you found yourself striving for something that wasn't truly aligned with your essence. How did it affect your peace and energy?
- If you were to stop "playing games" in your life right now, what would that truly mean for you? How might your daily actions, relationships, and priorities shift if you fully embraced living your Ikigai instead of striving for external markers of success?
- Think about a moment when you experienced effortless effort, similar to my AFTA training experience. How did it feel different from times of striving?
- How might embracing your Ikigai change your response to obstacles or challenges in your life, like my experience with Top Stern?
- What small step could you take today to expand your "20%"—the time and space where you most fully express your essence and purpose?

As you sit with these reflections, remember: your essence and purpose are already within you, waiting to be lived. Not someday, not when everything's perfect, but right now, in whatever you do. In the next chapter, we'll explore why this matters now more than ever, and how to sustain it once you've begun.

18

The Urgency of Ikigai

Up to this point, you've experienced the gentle guidance of the Kaizen-minded encourager, the easy-going Dave who wants to support you in uncovering and living your Ikigai. Now, I need you to listen closely, as I momentarily step into the former United States Marine Corps Sergeant role.

Don't worry; there won't be any yelling. Instead, I want to convey a sense of intensity and urgency. While expressing your Ikigai should be a natural and effortless process, there is one area where urgency is crucial: the decision to start living your Ikigai today.

Too often we wait for the perfect timing or circumstances. When you begin, it becomes. Embracing the journey as it unfolds allows us to find fulfillment and meaning in the unpredictable and incomplete. Coddiwomple isn't merely about traveling without a detailed road map; it's about purposefully embracing the exquisite unpredictability of life.

By giving up the need for perfect information or a painstakingly planned route, we unlock the door to many opportunities. It fosters a spirit of adventure, where the unforeseen becomes a benefit rather than a hindrance.

Possibilities abound in the uncertainties, gaps, and vague destinations that coddiwomple encourages us to explore. The catch is that it happens only when you start.

This next story is difficult for me to share, the reason for which you will realize as you read it. I'm going to recount this even with that difficulty in hopes it gives you the same sense of the urgency for Ikigai that it gave me.

An Unexpected Opportunity

The call was unexpected. Tim[1] was an executive VP of a large department where I worked. He was interested in creating a continuous improvement and innovation program. Several people in the company told him about my background in leading innovation and improvement transformations at other Fortune 500 companies. He invited me to lunch to discuss the programs I had started.

We met on a Friday, and he asked me how I would create such a program from scratch. I shared things like my Metavante story and others I had led before adding how I might modify the approach to fit the company's culture. The following Monday came the unexpected call.

"Would you like that job?" asked Tim.

"What job?"

"The one we talked about at lunch," was his reply.

In having a lunch conversation my only thought was to encourage him to create a continuous improvement program; running it never crossed my mind. I was in a secure senior position in IT. Taking this role would be a leap into the unknown. If the program failed, I could be out of a job with limited possibilities to return to IT at this or other companies.

So naturally, I said . . .

Yes!

Even though it was an undefined role with significant career risks, it aligned with my purpose. Purposefully moving toward a vague destination, I embraced coddiwomple and ultimately created a globally recognized continuous improvement program and in the process created my dream job.

Before that success could come, I had to prove myself and a program to a company that wasn't sure it needed either one. That's when I met John.

John was an employee in Tim's department and had been doing ad hoc continuous improvement work on his own for some time. As I mentioned earlier, this "program" I was starting wasn't funded.

The position had no job description or budget, and they were basically asking me to make it up as I went along. Tim thought it would be good if John was available to lend me a hand in getting started.

We Are Already Doing It!

John and I were opposites in virtually every aspect of our lives. From our philosophical beliefs and political leanings to our interests and lifestyles, we stood at opposite ends of the spectrum.

One thing we did share was a passion to make things better through continuous improvement. However, John believed there was no need for my involvement as he was already actively engaged in this work, and he let me know in no uncertain terms.

I invited John to lunch and asked him to tell me about the work he'd been doing. "Well, you know, I work with these teams, and I write some software or create some automation to help them out." He explained that for this one team, he had built an app to automate their process.

"Great," I said, "after lunch let's go take a look at it."

John was bright and capable and well liked in the department. He could be a huge asset to the program if he was on board. With his strong desire to make things better for others and the skills to back it up, this could also become a dream job for him. It was going to take some convincing on my part.

We visited the support team he had mentioned at lunch. When we arrived, everyone was heads down, working feverishly on the phone with customers. The manager, Sue, was excited to see John and greeted him with a hug. Above the cacophony of noise she said that, yes, they had used the app John created for them.

Then she paused and said, "But that was like a year ago, and I don't think we use it anymore. The team has gone back to doing things like they did before."

We visited another team with the same story, and yet another where it was the same. Over and over again, throughout the department, all of the things that John had created were used for a while then discontinued.

When they got busy, teams went back to the old ways of doing things. I explained to John that what we needed to do was build a system that was sustainable. One that allows us to improve and then keep improving.

Providing an Example

Years before, I had taken over a team that was in such a bad state that people warned me against taking on the role. They assured me it would ruin my career. In reality they were a hardworking group who had little to no leadership support, burdened by terrible systems and processes.

It might not surprise you to know that the process I started with was getting the noise down. Much like in the previous examples I've shared, once the noise level was reduced, we reinvested the time, energy, and focus on creating the virtuous cycle of continuous improvement.

It took a while but eventually we improved everything on the team, including their reputation. It became a highly successful group and model for others to follow.

I introduced John to the group and then asked some of them to demonstrate how we had worked together and established a system of improvement. He was amazed at the transformation, especially since he had heard about the team's poor reputation from years ago.

Then I pointed out I hadn't managed that team for about three years. Yet everything that I had done with them was still in place and had been improved even more since I left.

Then he got this gleam in his eye, like, "Oh, now I get it!"

It was an especially cool moment because it represented a break-through between us on a personal level. He hadn't trusted me before and couldn't see how I was going to accomplish the things I said I wanted to do. Now here was an entire team of people raving about the work I had led and how it had changed not only the work but their careers and personal lives as well.

It was also a poignant moment of realization for him because helping people was where his heart was really at. He wanted to make that kind of sustainable change and impact.

Bad News

Sadly, John and I didn't work together very long. In fact, two weeks after that "aha" moment, he got some bad news. He had colon cancer.

John was only 38 years old—far too young for colon cancer to be expected. At the time, routine screening for colon cancer wasn't even recommended until age 50, highlighting how unusual and tragic his diagnosis was. (It's worth noting that nowadays, guidelines suggest starting screenings a bit earlier, but still well beyond John's age at diagnosis.)

John and I got to know each other through texting. Because I was his boss, there were some work-related things around medical coverage and disability I had to communicate, which prompted our initial conversations. Over time, we connected in a more personal way. He was becoming too weak to talk on the phone so for many of those months we would text every day.

At one point John texted, "It's not looking good. You can feel free to shut down my phone and give my desk to someone else. It's unlikely I will return."

"No need my friend. If it is up to me, I am keeping your desk as it is." He never returned to work, and 15 months after his diagnosis, he was gone.

Empty Desk

The HR director and I had the responsibility of cleaning out his desk and boxing things up for John's family. He had been with the company for 18 years and all it took was 90 minutes to clear his desk. The next day I came into work and someone else was sitting there.

A Sense of Urgency

Though more than a decade ago, the lesson of John's passing has remained in my heart. Life is short. We only have now, and nothing guarantees tomorrow. John died with much of his song unplayed.

While uncovering and living your Ikigai is a lifelong pursuit, that doesn't mean you should postpone its beginning. The truth is, we never know how much time we have on this Earth, and every moment we spend not aligned with our essence and purpose is a moment we can never reclaim.

Not only that, think of Uzumaki, the concept of an ever-refined understanding represented by the swirl. The sooner you start, the sooner you will get to those inner rings of insight and living your Ikigai.

It's easy to get caught up in the day-to-day demands of life, to put off the work of self-discovery and alignment for another time. But the reality is, there will never be a perfect moment to start living your Ikigai. The only moment you have is now.

Approach the practices and principles of Ikigai with a spirit of ease and self-compassion, mixed with a sense of urgency and determination. Because the world needs the unique gifts and contributions that only you can offer, and every day you wait is a day that your light remains hidden. This is part of my drive to share Ikigai.

Living into that purpose is your irreplaceable expression of gifts, passions, skills, and place to impact the world. There's only one of us in all of time and creation. This unique expression will never exist again. That's why it's essential to live your Ikigai.

Sustainability

There was another crucial lesson from the tragedy of John's story. For a change to truly matter, for it to be transformative, it must be sustainable. It's not enough to simply make temporary improvements—the change must become ingrained and endure.

This truth of this is illustrated by the very team that provided John his "aha" moment of the importance of sustainable change. When we visited my old team, it had been years since I had been their leader, and I was only in charge of that team for two years. Yet the principles of continuous improvement, focused presence, and purposeful living they embodied outlasted my time on the team.

In the intervening years, many of the team members moved into leadership positions themselves and took the lessons with them. Recently, one former team member who has since retired reached out to share that the lessons learned during that time have had a lasting impact. Not only did she apply them throughout her career and ingrain them into her own teams, but they enhanced her personal life as well.

When the changes you seed are so durable that they become integrated into someone's very being and way of living, transcending any single role or circumstance—that is true sustainability. It's the difference between a fleeting work project and fundamentally altering the trajectory of a life for the better.

In my consulting practice I'll often put up a poster in the areas I'm working in that says . . . **There is no change if you don't sustain**.

This sobering truth was the crux of John's "aha" moment. He realized all the work he had done to make things better in his department was ultimately for naught because it didn't last. It lacked true sustainability. This revealed an inherent aspect of Kaizen—that whatever positive change you seek must be implemented in a way that fosters durable transformation in your life.

The commonly depicted Venn diagram model of Ikigai falls short in this regard. Firstly, by being overly focused on career. As you've learned over the course of this book, purpose is more than profession. Careers inevitably change, but your Ikigai should be an enduring core. Secondly, it is virtually impossible to find something you are passionate about, skilled at, and can be paid for 100% of the time. Life and interests are too dynamic for such rigid boundaries.

In contrast, the Three Invitations of Ikigai are inherently sustainable. They create a structure and system to support you in cultivating an environment that nurtures and grows your change. And, let's be real, living Ikigai IS a change. You can always express your essence and purpose in whatever your do. That is true sustainability. Moreover, the sooner you start, the more easily it is to start small.

Ultimate Frisbee and Potbellied Pigs

One of the best examples I've seen of someone truly living the sustainable Ikigai approach is my friend James Breakwell, who I've gotten to know recently. His full embrace of an urgency to uncover and express who he is in harmony with whatever he does is impressive.

202 THE IKIGAI WAY

James is a loving husband, dad to four young daughters under 13, a published author with a growing writing career; he cares for two pot-bellied pigs, and still shows up for a regular "day job." On top of all that, he has a Twitter (now known as X) account with over a million followers, where he jokingly refers to himself as "Twitter famous." Yet he does it all with a sense of flow, purpose, and presence that is inspiring and, most of all, sustainable.

James was 38, coincidentally the same age as John, when he came to this insight. "I've kind of got a new standard for what I keep in my life and what I get rid of. And it's just, do I watch the clock when I'm doing it? I got to the point where it's like, I can't, I can't wait till the kids are grown to start doing things, to start prioritizing stuff. I've got to live my life now. I've got to, you know, test out hobbies, do different things. For a while I joined a lot of things. I spread my claws kind of wide. And then after a while, a couple of years, I started looking at it and thought, 'Which of these things do I actually like, and which of these things am I doing just because I signed up for them?' And that was, that was my standard."[2]

James's approach to finding a sustainable way of living began with a willingness to experiment and try new things. This openness to new experiences allowed him to discover which activities truly resonated with his essence and purpose.

However, James didn't just stick with every new pursuit he tried. Instead, he developed a simple litmus test to determine which activities were worth continuing and which ones he needed to let go of. "If it was something that if I was watching the clock to get out of there, then, I didn't do it anymore," he shared. This self-reflective approach helped James grow what I call his Ikigai 20%.

As he describes it, "It's like, what do I actually enjoy and get lost in the flow of? Or like when I'm writing a newsletter, you know, you sit down and you get started. It doesn't matter how long it takes, you just write till it's done and you get in the flow of it."

James experimented, refined, and defined his purpose and created a system that works for him. That is the foundation of a sustainable approach. Having gotten to know James, I can tell you that he is spending more time in his 20% space than most. Imagine being able to have wonderful loving relationships, express your creativity at a high level, have unique hobbies like raising potbellied pigs, *AND* do all of it with a day job?

That last point is critical. James is the author of seven books. Seven! He someday hopes to make his entire living from his creative pursuits. Today, he has a regular job in addition to his creative work.

That is going to be true for most of us. The Venn Garden version of Ikigai misleads us. I don't know anyone in their late 30s more aligned with their Ikigai than James. And he has a day job.

The day job is almost certainly aligned with aspects of his life. While not explicitly his Ikigai, it isn't out of harmony with who he is or his purpose. We don't want a soul-crushing job and yet many of our most creative parts of our true selves will not generate all our income, and that is okay.

Your art is your art, whether you are making money from it or not. There is a difference being making a living as a creator and creating for a living.

James's example illustrates what it means to cultivate a sustainable approach to living one's Ikigai. It doesn't require quitting your job or radically upending your life all at once. Instead, it's an ongoing journey of experimentation, self-reflection, and crafting personalized systems that harmonize your various roles, responsibilities, and creative outlets. By being attuned to where he finds that sense of flow and purposeful engagement, James has masterfully woven his Ikigai through all facets of his life. His approach is dynamic yet enduring—the very essence of sustainability.

I do hope James eventually makes his living entirely from his creative pursuits. In part because he is immensely funny, and the world needs more wry humor. Also, because he and his wife will soon have four daughters all in their teens and I heard he's added a third potbellied pig.

If Not Now, When?

As we finish the penultimate chapter of this book, this thought from C. S. Lewis springs to mind: "The Future is something which everyone reaches at the rate of sixty minutes an hour, whatever he does, whoever he is."[3]

As Lewis reminds us, no one gets any special privilege regarding the future. We are all getting there at the same time. The difference, of course, is in what we do along the way. If you take a typical lifespan today, you get about **30,000** days of adult life, give or take. If you break it up, the first **10,000** ends as you move toward 30, the second middle to late 50s.

Those in their 50s are embarking on what will likely be their third and final segment of 10,000. I'm a little into that third **10,000**. I like to say I'm **mid-century modern**. It sounds so much cooler than 60.

Something about the framing of 10,000-day eras gives it importance over age or a random point in life. It gave me an even greater sense of urgency about embracing my Ikigai. John's death, barely past his first 10,000 days, gave me an even greater impetus to live into why I am here.

There is a reason you are here. As Buckminster Fuller expresses so eloquently, "Never forget that you are one of a kind. Never forget that if there weren't any need for you in all your uniqueness to be on this earth, you wouldn't be here in the first place. And never forget, no matter how overwhelming life's challenges and problems seem to be, that one person can make a difference in the world. In fact, it is always because of one person that all the changes that matter in the world come about. So be that one person."[4]

I'll change only one thing in Fuller's admonition. I say remember rather than "don't forget" (as Fuller does) because people do the command word. When you say, don't forget, the command word is "forget," and that's what the brain focuses on. That's a compelling example of a sustainable approach. The nature of our lives is made real by the language we use. When our words reflect what we want to do rather than what we don't want to do, we create a positive feedback loop that supports that behavior.

Remember that the unique expression of you will never happen again in all of time and space. Remember that tomorrow is not promised. And remember that if you want to fully live into you as a unique creation and fulfill your unique mission, you have to start small so you can sustain the gain and the change that comes from living your Ikigai.

Reflection

You may have noticed I didn't provide a numbered checklist or explicit "10 steps" for sustaining your Ikigai. Similarly, I consciously chose not to provide a formulaic process for cultivating urgency. This was intentional. Just as the rigid Venn diagram model fails to fully capture the essence of finding your purpose, prescribing a universal set of practices would undermine the inherently unique nature of each person's path to Ikigai.

Throughout this book, I "planted seeds" of ideas and practices that can create a sense of urgency and nurture sustainability for you. To support you further, here is one more "seed" I'm planting for harvest at the end of the next chapter. A single question to cultivate and sustain your personal spark of Ikigai.

How alive are you willing to be?[5]

19

Living the Question

"Those who are willing to be vulnerable move among mysteries."
—Theodore Roethke[1]

ANCIENT CHRISTIAN TRADITION speaks to working out our own salvation with fear and trembling. Which is to mean each in their own unique way with great seriousness and reverence for the process. It is much the same with Ikigai.

My Ikigai is not your Ikigai. The way I come to live out mine may not be the way you live out yours. My aim in writing this book has been to fill the role of mystagogue, someone who initiates others into beliefs and teachings, often associated with hidden wisdom and sacred mysteries.

I've carefully crafted this book to provide wayfinding without being overly prescriptive. What I've given you serves as a framework, a guide, and a means to uncover and live out your own unique reason for being. You are not a problem to be solved or fixed, rather a mystery to be lived. My role has been to lead you into the deeper mystery of Ikigai, opening you up to the world of possibilities and purpose.

The best way to explore that world is through questions. It is one reason I refer to Ikigai as a quest. Quest is the root word of question. Questions become our tools for exploration and provide both the quickening and answer to our mysteries. Remember, if you can ask yourself questions, you can uncover your purpose, even if you have no idea what you are called to do today.

Our quest to uncover Ikigai began with the three fundamental questions each of us seeks to answer.

- Who am I?
- Why am I here?
- What should I do?

Like many things in life, those questions are both too simple and too complex to answer at the beginning of your quest. That's why I created a framework and approach that allows you to go from simple to complex in answering those questions.

Kaizen and Complexity

We need both simple and complex systems in life. Even though we need both, the best design is to be as simple as possible and then no simpler. A pencil for example is quite simple and yet we can't do with it what we can with a laptop. Make things as simple as possible while still capable of doing what we need them to do.

Answering those three foundation questions is hard. A Kaizen approach is about breaking down those questions into the smallest and simplest form possible in the beginning and adding in complexity only as understanding increases.

Ikigai isn't the all too simple answer of what you do for a living. While simple, it doesn't provide a foundation for exploring and developing a richer understanding. Your Ikigai is the far more complex and nuanced experience of who you are, why you are here, expressed in harmony with whatever you do.

Complex understanding such as this must be grown from simple systems that already work or are understood. Not complexity for complexity's sake and not complexity at the start but built on functioning systems and practices.

Simplicity is often misunderstood. We need systems and processes that can do many things, some of which are complex. They should be as elegant and simple as possible while still delivering all that we need. Growing the "complexity" from simply working systems is a way to ensure just such an outcome.

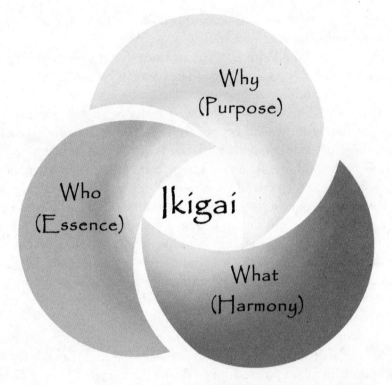

Figure 19.1   The Who, What, and Why of life, answered by Ikigai.

That is why we began with understanding what Ikigai is at the foundation level. It's why we identified and created a framework for answering those three fundamental questions with Ikigai.

The Who, What, and Why of life are answered with the who (essence), why (purpose), and what (harmony) of Ikigai (see Figure 19.1).

The simple understanding of that framework enabled you to begin your quest by accepting the Three Invitations.

1. Getting the Noise Down.
2. Uncovering your Purpose.
3. Living your Ikigai.

These three simple invitations offer opportunities to create working systems, processes, and understanding. By accepting them, you open yourself to a more complex exploration of who you are at your deepest levels, why you are here, and how you can express both in harmony with whatever you do.

Do you recall the Venn Garden? I warned that starting with it leads many people away from their Ikigai. The reason is because it attempts to build a complex understanding on systems that are failing.

The great irony I shared with you early on was by focusing on career at the outset you all but guaranteed you wouldn't find a career that supported your Ikigai. Instead, the Ikigai Way is to begin by first getting the noise down. Then next, reinvesting the capacity generated by noise reduction to create a simple working model of your purpose, your Ikiverse. From there beginning the exploration of who you really are under all the debris life has laid on top of your essence.

The system of noise reduction followed by creating working systems to move the flywheel of a virtuous cycle is the ultimate simple to complex approach. You can apply this to any area and situation in your life. It works as well with individuals as it does families or even giant global companies.

As simple as you can in the beginning, so that you develop working systems that support you moving up the value chain of understanding and of life. The progression from simple to complex isn't only a theoretical model; you've experienced the transition of simple working systems to complex systems in your life before.

Child–Camel–Lion . . . and Child Again

Remember the allegory in the Prologue? It represented such a change and perfectly illustrates how we have navigated these transitions throughout our lives. We start as that child exploring the world around us with a natural curiosity. We take our simple understanding and grow by establishing working systems of understanding to take on an ever more complex approach to life.

Then the world starts adding systems. There are lessons taught and burdens placed so we can operate in society. Go to school, get a job, and all the rest. Learning the ways of life, our essence gets covered as we transition to being a camel to bear the ever-heavier burdens of life.

At some point those systems made by the world quit working, no longer allowing the growth we need. We wonder if there is more all the while trudging on accepting the "thou shalts" structuring our lives around failing systems. This makes life complicated, not complex. Failed rather than elegant, frustrating instead of filled with flow.

An Aha Moment

Like the lion, we all reach that point where what served us for so long no longer does. When I experienced this point in my own life, I was fortunate enough to have a life-changing epiphany triggered by a lateral thinking puzzle. Lateral Thinking[2] is a problem-solving approach that encourages viewing challenges from unconventional angles. Little did I know, this seemingly simple exercise would lead to a profound realization about my own situation.

The puzzle starts with six pieces, numbered 1–6. The challenge is to add one piece at a time in numerical order, with each addition forming a recognizable shape—a square, rectangle, trapezoid, or combination.

At first, it seems straightforward. Pieces 1 and 2, three flat sides and one angled side, placed together easily form a square. Adding the third piece creates a rectangle. As you progress, each new piece slots in, creating increasingly complex shapes. It seems almost too easy until you come to the final piece—a long parallelogram that simply won't fit into the carefully constructed pattern you've built.

Here's the twist: to complete the puzzle, you must start over. The only solution is to take everything apart and begin again, this time placing pieces 1 and 2 as a parallelogram. From this new foundation, each subsequent piece falls into place, culminating in a perfect fit for that challenging sixth piece.

Like most people who do this puzzle, I tried moving a few pieces here to there, reformatting what was already in place. My mind was locked into the initial pattern of a square. The tyranny of the existing locks us all into old habits, beliefs, and behaviors.

Solving this puzzle mirrors our Ikigai journey. It isn't until we drop all our preconceptions that we can see a new way. Often, we build our lives piece by piece, following societal norms and expectations. We create a structure that seems logical, even impressive. But when we try to add that final piece—our Ikigai—we find it doesn't fit the life we've constructed.

We must return to our essence, our "child" state, and reconstruct our lives from that authentic foundation. It's a powerful reminder that how we start often determines our path, and reaching our ultimate outcome may require breaking down the systems we've built to create something truer to ourselves. But like the lion turning into the child, you return to simple working systems and rebuild, only this time you do so with all the experience and wisdom of the life you've already lived. You create a working system from scratch that, like the parallelogram, supports who you are at your deepest levels, your gifts, passions and purpose lived out this time in harmony with all that you do.

Think back to the Three Invitations. Through the seven rituals you begin the process of getting the noise down in your life—the first invitation. You have examples, such as "deleting the line" of how you can create and grow your own methods for reducing noise in every area of life.

With the noise level down the flywheel starts moving. You take the capacity that was wasted in dealing with noise and reinvest it in uncovering your purpose—the second invitation. Creating your purpose statement with your Ikiverse then enables you to explore and to go deeper into understanding your purpose. Through that exploration you begin the uncovering of your essence, who you really are, who that person was way back before the world told you who you were.

And finally, you've been introduced to sustainability—the piece that brings it all together. You've learned how to start this flywheel, and how to accelerate the virtuous cycle it represents. Through sustainability, you'll keep it spinning as more and more of your life is experienced in your Ikigai—the third invitation.

The Incomplete Guide

I'll share a secret with you. My original title for this book was "The Incomplete Guide to a Life of Purpose." In part because there is no way to write a single book that answers everything for you.

In my decades of supporting people transforming their lives and businesses, I've learned that dramatic positive change rarely happens when I simply tell people what to do. Instead, it occurs when I create opportunities for them to uncover insights themselves. That is the whole point of this quest—for you to uncover your own Ikigai. No one can do it for you, and no one else's journey will be exactly like yours.

My intention is to initiate you into your understanding of Ikigai, giving you wayfinders and approaches that speed you along the path equipped with understanding, systems, rituals, and processes to provide you with your own potent "aha" moments. From there, you build on them to create your more complex understanding of your Ikigai, your Uzumaki.

Armed with your Ikiverse, you have already shaved off years of philosophical wandering—a journey that took me decades to navigate. The lessons shared here further accelerate you on your path. You now have everything you need to live fully into your Ikigai, to live out the life you were created for.

Only one thing remains. Throughout this book, we've explored the power of questions to uncover truths and spark transformation. In the previous chapter, I planted a seed with a question. The right questions lead us to our answers, and this one is perhaps the most transformative of all.

"How alive am I willing to be?"

Your answer to this question, and how it evolves over time, will guide you toward a life of ever-deepening purpose and fulfillment. The journey begins with your willingness to ask and continues with your courage to live the answer.

Begin and it becomes. Quest well.

Notes

Chapter 1

1. Inspired by Friedrich Nietzsche, *Thus Spake Zarathustra: A Book for All and None*, trans. Thomas Common (Digireads, 2016).
2. While widely attributed to Meister Eckhart no source document can be sited. Common attribution is by John O'Donohue during an interview, On Being with Krista Tippett, accessed September 26, 2024, https://onbeing.org/programs/john-odonohue-the-inner-landscape-of-beauty
3. Default, n. v., "Online Etymology Dictionary," accessed May 20, 2024, https://www.etymonline.com/word/default#etymonline_v_42075
4. Carol Hymowitz, "Older Workers Have a Big Secret: Their Age," *Wall Street Journal*, November 17, 2019.
5. "Can you remember who you were, before the world told you who you should be?"— Little Books of Wisdom, Charles Bukowski, *A Little Book of Essential Quotes on Life, Art, and Love*.

Chapter 2

1. Some names and identifying details have been changed to protect the privacy of individuals.
2. Ken played an essential role in my Ikigai journey, which is shared in more detail in the Acknowledgments section. He also introduced me to Adam Hansen, whose guidance was instrumental in the early stages of my exploration.

Chapter 3

1. R. Buckminster Fuller, "The Comprehensive Man," in *R. Buckminster Fuller on Education*, ed. Peter H. Wagschal and Robert D. Kahn (Amherst: University of Massachusetts Press, 1979), 77.
2. This saying is often attributed to Mark Twain, though there is no record of him ever having said it. It is regarded as a common saying with an anonymous originator. "Two Most Important Days in Your Life: Origin of a Mark Twain Quotation," *Quote Investigator*, accessed September 26, 2024, https://quoteinvestigator.com/2016/06/22/why
3. Visier. (2021). Survey Finds 70% of Burnt Out Employees Would Leave Job, accessed September 26, 2024, https://www.visier.com/blog/new-survey-70-percent-burnt-out-employees-would-leave-current-job

Chapter 4

1. Anne Lamott, *Small Victories: Spotting Improbable Moments of Grace* (New York: Riverhead Books, 2014), 149.
2. Marc Parent, "Learning to Run Farther Than Seemed Possible," *Runner's World*, March 18, 2013, accessed September 26, 2024, https://www.runnersworld.com/runners-stories/a20838177/learning-to-run-farther-than-seemed-possible

Chapter 6

1. Not his real name and some details are changed to protect privacy.

Chapter 7

1. While often attributed to Albert Einstein, there's no evidence he actually said this. Nonetheless, the sentiment captures an important idea about the relationship between understanding and clear communication.
2. Steven Pressfield, *The War of Art* (New York: Black Irish Entertainment LLC, 2002), 146.
3. Not her real name, identifying details have been changed

Chapter 9

1. Name and some identifying elements changed for privacy.
2. Names and some identifying elements changed for privacy.

Chapter 10

1. George E. P. Box, Alberto Luceño, and María del Carmen Paniagua-Quiñones, *Statistical Control By Monitoring and Adjustment*. 2nd ed. (Hoboken, NJ: John Wiley & Sons, 2009), 61.
2. No original source can be identified; the quote is consistently attributed to Thomas Merton across multiple references.
3. John Wilson, interview in "The Woodworker," episode 1, season 1, A Craftsman's Legacy, produced by Hammer in Hand Productions, accessed July 2, 2024, www.craftsmanslegacy.com.
4. *Let Your Life Speak: Listening for the Voice of Vocation* (San Francisco: Jossey-Bass), 38.
5. Not his real name.
6. This quote is commonly attributed to Cocteau in various collections of quotations though original source reference is given.

Chapter 11

1. Masters & Masterworks Productions, Inc. All rights reserved.

Chapter 12

1. Lao Tzu, *Tao Te Ching*.

Chapter 13

1. Dictionary.com, s.v. "harmony" (n.), accessed July 5, 2024, https://www.dictionary.com/browse/harmony
2. George Martine, ed., *The New Global Frontier: Urbanization, Poverty and Environment in the 21st Century* (London: Taylor & Francis Group, 2008), 141.
3. M. J. Ryan, ed., *The Fabric of the Future: Women Visionaries of Today Illuminate the Path to Tomorrow* (Berkeley, CA: Conari Press, 1998), 3.
4. I use only my grandchildren's first initial to protect their privacy.

5. Principle Financial "Dream Car" commercial, accessed October 2, 2024, https://vimeo.com/326919547
6. King James Version, Ecclesiastes 3:1.
7. Nouwen, Henri, *Out of Solitude: Three Meditations on the Christian Life* (Notre Dame, IN: Ave Maria Press), 1974.

Chapter 14

1. Dieter Rams, "Dieter Rams: Less and More Interview," interview by Gestalten, Vimeo video, accessed July 5, 2024, https://vimeo.com/7917568

Chapter 15

1. Cheri Huber. AZQuotes.com, Wind and Fly LTD, 2024. https://www.azquotes.com/quote/1397617, accessed July 6, 2024.
2. Scripture quotations marked (NIV) are taken from the Holy Bible, New International Version®, NIV®. Copyright © 1973, 1978, 1984, 2011 by Biblica, Inc.™ Used by permission of Zondervan. All rights reserved worldwide. www.zondervan.com. The "NIV" and "New International Version" are trademarks registered in the United States Patent and Trademark Office by Biblica, Inc.™

Chapter 16

1. Adam L. Alter and Hal E. Hershfield, "People Search for Meaning When They Approach a New Decade in Chronological Age," *Proceedings of the National Academy of Sciences* 111, no. 48 (2014): 17066–17070, https://www.pnas.org/doi/10.1073/pnas.1415086111
2. Name changed for privacy.
3. Edward Slingerland, *Trying Not to Try: The Art and Science of Spontaneity* (New York: Crown, 2014).
4. Mihaly Csikszentmihalyi, *Flow: The Psychology of Optimal Experience* (New York: Harper & Row, 1990).

Chapter 17

1. Scripture quotations are taken from the Holy Bible, New Living Translation, copyright © 1996, 2004, 2015 by Tyndale House Foundation. Used by permission of Tyndale House Publishers, Carol Stream, Illinois 60188. All rights reserved.

2. Name and some identifying characteristics changed for privacy.
3. Sergeant Major: The highest-ranking enlisted position in the Marine Corps.
4. Not his real name.

Chapter 18

1. Name and some identifying details have been changed to protect privacy.
2. David Marlow, "Episode 1," Podquest, Ikiquest (podcast), December 11, 2023, https://ikiquest.substack.com/p/podquest-episode-1-912, accessed October 3, 2024.
3. C.S. Lewis, "Quote by C.S. Lewis: 'The future is something which everyone reaches . . .'" Goodreads. Accessed September 9, 2024. https://www.goodreads.com/quotes, accessed October 3, 2024.
4. R. Buckminster Fuller. "Never forget that you are one of a kind. . ." This quote is widely attributed to Fuller on various websites and in popular media, but no primary source has been identified.
5. Inspired by Anne Lamott, "This business of becoming conscious, of being a writer, is ultimately about asking yourself, as my friend Dale puts it, How alive am I willing to be?" *The Quotable Book Lover* (United States: Skyhorse, 2013).

Chapter 19

1. Theodore Roethke, *The Collected Poems of Theodore Roethke* (Seattle, WA: University of Washington Press, 1982).
2. Edward De Bono, *Lateral Thinking: Creativity Step by Step* (New York: Harper & Row, 1970), 32.

Acknowledgments

NEARLY A DECADE ago, when my corporate career took an unexpected turn, I decided to become active on LinkedIn, sharing ideas without any specific agenda. This unplanned journey led me to explore the concept of Ikigai, thanks to a suggestion from my respected friend and talented writer, Ken Gordon.

As I delved deeper into Ikigai, I found it encapsulated everything I wanted to do—living out my purpose while helping others uncover theirs. Years of research, writing, and coaching others on this topic followed, gradually establishing me as a recognized authority on Ikigai. Ken even dubbed me "The Ikigai Guy," a title that brought both notoriety and unexpected opportunities.

One such opportunity came in the form of an email from Victoria Savannah, an assignment editor at a major publishing firm, expressing interest in me writing a book on Ikigai. Initially skeptical, I nearly missed this chance by ignoring the email, thinking it was spam. Fortunately, Victoria's patience and persistence paid off, and after months of refining the concept, I received the green light to write this book.

Throughout this process, I've come to appreciate King Solomon's timeless observation that "there is nothing new under the sun."

I've gained an understanding of the wisdom in this saying, and this book is proof of it in action. There is nothing ever completely unique and new. Everything is built out of some combination of what has come before.

The *new* if there is any is in the combining of ideas, insights, and wisdom that already exist in unique ways. As such, it is my hope this book has provided a useful new combination from what I have learned along the way. I'm deeply indebted to the numerous thinkers and practitioners across various fields—including philosophy, psychology, management, and creativity—whose work has profoundly influenced my own.

Special thanks go to Brian Kempton, my coach, mentor, and friend, whose guidance encouraged me to live out my own calling and share this unique approach to Ikigai.

To my friends who have been part of this journey: your support, patience, and encouragement have been my constant companions. While I can't name each of you here, as you read these words, I hope you see your own unique contribution reflected throughout the pages of this book.

My heartfelt gratitude extends to my family, especially my adult children and grandchildren. My life is blessed beyond what I can express here because of each one of you. Your love, encouragement, and inspiration remind me daily what truly matters in life.

Above all, I must acknowledge my wife, Alicia. For over 40 years, she has stood by my side, supporting my dream of being a writer even when I doubted myself. Her unwavering belief in me has been the foundation of everything I've achieved. This book, like all the good in my life, owes so much to her presence. Thank you, my love, for being my constant companion on this incredible journey.

To Victoria and the team at Wiley, thank you for your vision and for this extraordinary opportunity to share Ikigai. It's not lost on me how unusual and blessed I am to have been approached to write this book, rather than the other way around.

About the Author

DAVID MARLOW EMBARKED on an extraordinary journey after a 30-year career as a senior leader and executive in three Fortune 500 companies. Seizing an opportunity to leave corporate life, Dave pursued his true calling: championing people and businesses in finding fulfillment and living their purpose. Through coaching, consulting, and mentoring, he supports individuals in transforming their lives and careers while guiding companies to infuse purpose into their products and people.

A globally recognized expert, his powerful messages have reached millions through his work, widely shared articles, and popular newsletter Ikiquest, offering ideas, insights, and stories that inspire. Dave's unique approach combines the quest for personal fulfillment with the practical application of purpose in careers and business, earning him the moniker "The Ikigai Guy."

Now in his book, Dave is the first to explain how to express who you are and why you are here in harmony with whatever you do—cultivating a holistic understanding of purpose. Drawing from decades of studying personal transformation, he has created a unique framework enabling people to uncover their Ikigai.

When not empowering others to live purposefully, this self-proclaimed "mid-century modern" can be found sipping espresso, training for marathons, or enjoying time with his family. A devoted husband, father, and grandfather, Dave resides in Hartland, Wisconsin.

Visit davidmarlow.com for additional resources, insights, and opportunities to engage with Dave's work, including speaking events, coaching, and consulting services.

Index

Page numbers followed by *f* refer to figures.